LIFE IN COLOR

CULTURE IN AMERICAN PSYCHIATRY

Rodrigo Munoz, M.D.

Annelle Primm, M.D.

Jambur Ananth, M.D.

Pedro Ruiz, M.D.

HILTON PUBLISHING COMPANY · CHICAGO, ILLINOIS

Published by
Hilton Publishing Company, Inc.
1630 45th St., Ste. 103
Munster, IN 46321
815–885–1070
www.hiltonpub.com

Library of Congress Cataloging-in-Publication Data

Life in color : culture in American psychiatry / Rodrigo A. Munoz . . . [et al.].
    p. cm.
  Includes index.
  ISBN 0-9743144-9-8 (pbk. : alk. paper)
  1. Minorities—Mental health—United States. 2. Psychiatry, Transcultural.
3. Mental illness—United States—Cross-cultural studies. I. Munoz, Rodrigo A.
  RC451.5.A2L54 2005
  362.2'089—dc21   2005006571

Printed and bound in the United States of America

ISBN: 0–9743144–9–8

To Jambur Ananth, a wonderful colleague, friend and associate who was an exceptional clinician, researcher, administrator and a national leader of the minorities in psychiatry.

CONTENTS

CONTENTS

CULTURE AND CLINICAL PRACTICE

When we started conversations with Hilton Publishing about a book on cultural issues in psychiatry, we saw a golden opportunity to write one that could be relevant to the practicing clinician. Because we have sometimes been unhappy to read treatises on culture written as if they refer to faraway people we seldom see, we wanted the clinical psychiatrist to see his or her daily practice within the pages of our book. We wanted to talk about the most common disorders in a general psychiatric practice. We wanted to talk about them as they affect the members of minority groups.

When we began planning the book, it became abundantly clear that Chapter One, *Miami Blues*, should say what many are already witnessing: America is rapidly becoming a country of minorities. They bring with them all the cultural richness accumulated elsewhere over the centuries. America's variety is one of our main assets, which permits a continual flow of ideas, perceptions, attires, habits, and much more.

Chapter Two, *Tones of Blue*, and Chapter Three, *Tones of Indigo*, are devoted to depressive and anxiety disorders. This is so because these disorders, according to repeated surveys, represent about one half of the patients in a clinical psychiatry practice. Not only that.

They are common, easily diagnosable, and likely to be successfully treated. Yet they also may be accompanied by disability and/or death.

Currently, major depressive disorder (MDD) is a leading cause of disability in the United States. It has significant co-morbidity with many other conditions, including the metabolic syndrome x and cancer. Panic disorders and drug addiction also may be present in patients with MDD. One in six Americans will suffer from MDD at some point in their lives.

In a given year, approximately five percent of adults in the United States will suffer from depression. Further, MDD is the cause of a majority of suicides in one year. The total direct and indirect costs of depression have been estimated at between 40 and 80 billion dollars annually.

Though there is solid information that psychotherapy and antidepressants are 80 percent effective in people with depression, less than 25 percent of adults diagnosed with depression received treatment in 1997. We have a number of ideas and opinions about the reasons for this lack of treatment, especially among minority patients. The evidence and our reactions to it are presented in several chapters that address lack of access to care for minorities.

The cases we present in early chapters are examples of MDD occurring among minorities in diverse settings. We continue to regret that there are major barriers between the depressed person and the professionals prepared to help her. The barriers include the stigma that accompanies the psychiatric disorder, which is possibly worse among minorities. Financial problems also interfere. The busy family physician, minimally paid for each visit, may not be able to spend enough time with the patient to develop a detailed knowledge about the symptoms, their course, precipitating events, treatments the patient has had, her response to previous treatments, family history, and the potential risk of suicide. This matter is complicated by persistent deficits in primary-care training programs on the diagnosis and treatment of MDD.

INTRODUCTION

The first chapters also present the multiple permutations we observe between the depressive syndrome and a number of other disorders. Some of our patients have several diagnoses and need treatment for all of them. Bipolar disorder type II (BPII) is often difficult to diagnose because the patient may come for treatment only when she is depressed, and the periods of hypomania may be described as periods of excellent health. That depression may become the most urgent problem in a patient that is being treated for another disorder, tends to challenge the best treatment planners.

Manic and hypomanic episodes are increasingly being diagnosed in clinical practice. The clinical expression of a bipolar disorder may go from subtle mood swings to clear episodes of psychosis. The clinician may be baffled when an atypical presentation is tinged by cultural factors.

Anxiety disorders are very much present in most psychiatric clinical practices. Whether on their own or, more often, accompanied by other disorders, including depression, alcoholism, and many others, they may be missed. Considering that depression and anxiety disorders coincide in about half of the patients we see with either disorder, the clinician may want to always be prepared to diagnose and treat both.

Suicide is a permanent concern when treating patients with depression, alcoholism, other addictions, and many other psychiatric disorders. Many suicides occur among patients with a family and personal history of suicidal behavior. The clinician should always be interested in evaluating the patient's risk of suicide and establishing adequate preventive measures.

Depression occurs in children and in older persons. Today, more is known about childhood depression, and many psychiatrists are participating in the debate as to the best treatment programs. Geriatricians and other psychiatrists are seeing patients in their later years who suffer from depression. One of the major challenges in treating patients with dementing disorders is the successful treatment of coexistent depressions.

Chapter Four, *Twisting Reality*, explores the psychoses, with emphasis on schizophrenia. Any psychiatrist that treats chronically ill patients sees those who suffer long-term psychoses; these patients may not have funds for adequate evaluation and care, and they might have difficulty obtaining support for rehabilitation programs. Schizophrenia tends to drain sources of help, isolate the sufferer, and alienate many in her family. It is often the psychiatrist who has to negotiate the obstacles to family and social reintegration. Schizophrenia continues to be a major challenge in the struggle for better care for all of our patients.

Addictive disorders are addressed in Chapter Five, *Twilight Zone*. Alcoholism and all the other addictions continue to be a major concern for those dealing with minorities. We are often distressed because the deviant adolescent who uses drugs is often referred to the penal system, which contributes to the large presence of minority youths in jails and prisons. We try to demonstrate that we have effective therapeutic strategies to deal with addiction, and that we can be successful when given a chance. Any program that deals with care of minorities should try to, by necessity, include preventive and therapeutic measures for drug addiction.

Chapter Six, *Talking*, presents our perspective about the use of psychotherapy in the treatment of minority patients. We regret that some colleagues fail to understand that minority patients are receptive to psychotherapy, profit from it, and are better off because their therapists are skillful in verbal therapies. We have been gratified to observe the excellent results obtained by professionals using psychotherapy in the treatment of a large variety of psychiatric disorders among the minorities, more so as some patients were initially not considered good candidates. We would like more papers and more presentations on the psychotherapeutic needs of minority communities.

Chapter Seven, *Remedies in Color*, addresses a number of issues on the use of psychotropic compounds in the treatment of minority patients. Considering that both Drs. Ananth and Ruiz have written

INTRODUCTION

books on psychopharmacology, we had expected the chapter to be an easy one. This was not the case. The field has grown exponentially, new discoveries produce new areas of inquiry. Minorities are far from homogeneous, and almost any statement requires a number of explanations. We ended up with a robust chapter that, in our opinion, represents the state-of-the-art as of the time of publication.

We traveled around the United States collecting information for Chapter Eight, *Odysseys*, which presents our perceptions about the history of many ethnic groups in the United States. The recently opened National Museum of the American Indian was a major eye-opener about the history of a noble and generous people who were almost exterminated. The Hmong people and the Cuban Americans who migrated recently to the United States gave us very valuable insights. The autobiography of a distinguished African-American humanist whose life started in the time of intense discrimination was also very helpful. We ended up using just a fraction of the myriad of facts and thoughts we had collected. We came out from the writing with several new ideas. One of them is that the fate of minorities will hinge largely on their representation in the U.S. Congress.

Chapter Nine, *The Texture and Beauty of Color*, took advantage of Dr. Ananth's dedication to family studies throughout his professional life. (He had already written on the Indian Family.) Each of the authors contributed their personal knowledge and involvement in the many initiatives and programs that have been created in the last four decades to study and help the minority family. This is one area of study that will still develop and crystallize.

Chapter Ten, *Disparities*, was written at a time when the Institute of Medicine, the American Medical Association (AMA), the Office of the Surgeon General of the United States, the National Institutes of Health (NIH), and many other organizations are studying the reasons for disparities in the outcome of medical care among different groups. We would like to distribute the responsibility to include all of us, and insist that we, too, as representatives and leaders of the minorities, have a place in influencing all those who participate in health care, and to make things equal. Some of the deficiencies are in the way we minorities think and react. We have to develop an increasingly proactive attitude if we are going to advance.

Our plan for writing the book called for a close cooperation among authors who would be Latino, Asian, and African American. Long ago, I developed a profound skepticism about multi-authored books. I criticized them for being written in different styles, often with lack of continuity and many gaps. I proposed to Drs. Pedro Ruiz, Jambur Ananth, and Annelle Primm that we all participate in writing every chapter, so that we could have a cohesive and easy-to-follow narrative. If we succeeded, it was because of my co-authors' patience, interest, knowledge, and perseverance. If we failed, I take the responsibility.

Drs. Ruiz and Ananth have had extraordinary careers spanning a number of decades. They rapidly climbed key academic ladders early in their careers, and became seasoned administrators, researchers, teachers, and leaders. We were gratified to see Dr. Ruiz elected president of the American Psychiatric Association (APA) in 2004.

Last year the APA reopened its Office on Minorities and National Affairs. The position of director was offered to Dr. Annelle Primm, the youngest of our coauthors. Dr. Primm who excelled as a student at Harvard University and Howard University, has quickly advanced to positions of leadership at Johns Hopkins University, and is already a key community leader and minority advocate ready to lead us into the future. We are very pleased she agreed to join us in the writing of this book.

—*Rodrigo A. Munoz, M.D*

CHAPTER ONE

MIAMI BLUES

Stressors and Cultural Factors Among Ethnic Minority Groups in the United States

The city of Miami, Florida, has recently achieved a special distinction; at the present time, most of its residents are from countries other than the United States. Following a tradition that has been honored by most migration waves, the newcomers usually settle in places abandoned by those of the immediately preceding wave who have "moved up" in social status and financial security.

The recent "waves" have been far from homogeneous. Take, for example, Mr. Louis Petion, Ms. Estelita Brown, and Ms. Rafaela Lopez.

Mr. Louis Petion was a proud and very solemn Haitian, who told us that he came to the United States in a last effort to save his life. He had fallen victim to the "secret" attacks of unknown enemies who had drained all his energy and life from his brain and his heart. He was dead for all practical purposes. Additionally, he couldn't sleep or eat; he was becoming just flesh and bones; he couldn't think and he couldn't even fend for himself. Though he had firm suspicions about the possible perpetrators of the curse that was killing him, he didn't have enough knowledge of magic powers to protect himself. The suggestion that he could be suffering from an illness and, even worse, a mental illness, was absolutely and vigorously rejected; Mr. Petion was offended by such a ridiculous contention.

Ms. Estelita Brown, a petite and vivacious product of Manila, was the opposite. Following in the footsteps of two aunts and a sister, she had been preparing to start working as a nurse in a large hospital and wanted to be as successful as they were. When she started crying, losing weight, and having difficulty sleeping, Ms. Brown consulted her Aunt Mercedes—who had previously suffered a depression. She helped enroll Ms. Brown into an excellent treatment program. Currently, Ms. Brown is more than ready to talk about depression at length and for hours; she knows well that learning everything she could was at the center of her future success.

Ms. Rafaela Lopez originally from Mexico, was upset at the suggestion that she could possibly be depressed. Her reasoning: What did you expect? Hadn't the good Rogelio, her husband of forty years, died just three years before? Shouldn't she devote the rest of her life to crying and going religiously to the cemetery twice a week? And, now that her children had removed her from her beloved Mazatlan, Mexico, to bring her to this "Tower of Babel," shouldn't she feel worse? Ms. Lopez took suggestions of "getting psychotherapy" as attempts to minimize her loss and convert her pain into a treatable condition. As she wrote to a sister, "Children are not what they used to be. Instead of feeling compassion and offering love, they want to take you to a 'stranger doctor' to be given pills . . . as if they can't understand that you suffer because you have a broken heart."

As these three examples show, people are different, and they are also often different within each group. When a group shares similar norms and traditions, we say that the members of the group have the same "culture." And, as with many human affairs, it is easier to define "culture" than to define the actual behaviors inherent in each group. We are more confident in saying that African Americans, Asians, and Latinos are different from each other rather than defining the ways in which they are different, and the ways in which their behaviors are inherently different within each group.

There are a number of words that are used to define similar characteristics within the same group of individuals. We have decided not to use the words "race" and "ethnicity." The term "culture" seems big enough to include race and ethnicity without splitting too many hairs.* The following paragraphs offer our explanation.

RACE AND GRANULARITY

Those interested in a scientific definition need to recognize that the classification of race emerges from the analysis of the frequency of functional variants of genes encoding drug-metabolizing enzymes. This analysis has led to four clusters: Sub-Saharan Africa, Western Eurasia, China, and New Guinea, which have been converted into Africa, Eurasia, East Asia, Oceania, and America. (Note 1–1).

This neat schema is rendered less realistic by the existence of many exceptions to the geographic distribution of alleles, the many factors that influence drug response, and the "granular" (dispersed) distribution of genes in many areas. Thus, drug responses are more easily predicted in persons who come from China and less easily predicted in persons coming from the Pacific Rim.

As if this situation did not create formidable obstacles in the study of race, we also know that its relative influence needs to be studied in the context of educational levels, occupation, type of diet, place of residence, and environmental exposure. These factors combined with race affiliation have a reciprocal effect: they are affected by the individual's perceived race.

Ethnicity has mostly to do with inheritance and cultural factors with environmental influences. The relative value of each in a given group is difficult to determine; each influences the other and, unless

---

* We rapidly found that we could not stop using expressions such as "ethnic minority professionals" to mean that the physicians and the patients came from the same countries. "Ethnic minority care" means that the patient may be jeopardized by others' perceptions. We found that we can't stop using the word "ethnic" when we are talking about perceived unfairness to those who do not look as most of the people.

a study focuses on isolated populations, they may come together when attempting to research just one.

Finally, the genetic composition of each group continues to evolve, so that Cubans in the United States and Cubans from Cuba today have different proportions of African and Caucasian genetic representation.

WHAT IS CULTURAL?

We assume that cultural factors, including family beliefs, traditions, accepted perceptions of reality, and learned coping skills influenced the current belief systems of the people in the earlier examples: Mr. Petion, Ms. Brown, and Ms. Lopez. Early in life, we are subjected to ideas that go unquestioned in our communities and in our families. Depending on the traits that are considered desirable or problematic, helpful or destructive, we tend to identify with those who represent community ideals and cultural traditions as well. Thus, different communities will hold different archetypes in high esteem: warriors; merchants; priests; philosophers; poets, or still others who represent what is considered most valuable. The perceptions of reality are often subjected to adjustments, so that these community ideals are preserved even when they are no longer adaptive.

HEXING

Long before Mr. Petion arrived in Miami, the *American Journal of Psychiatry* (1–2) was publishing papers about hexing. "Conjure doctors," "the two-headed," "root doctors," and "voodoo men" have been reported as supposedly capable of "tricking" or hexing a person to produce sickness, insanity, and even death. This belief presumably came to Haiti and Louisiana from West Africa early in the eighteenth century. In areas where hexing is an accepted belief, it is accompanied by symptoms suggestive of depression, which may often advance the victim's demise. In this context, family and friends withdraw their support, and the sufferer becomes an outsider.

No wonder Mr. Petion chose to migrate. He was a man who was respected and even loved in his poor community, a place with strong beliefs in incantations, curses, and influence through magical means. Mr. Petion supported these beliefs that mixed magic with reality; he too gave value to perceptions that justified these beliefs—even when they represented distortions of actual events. Thus, when Mr. Petion, a beloved pillar of the community, became depressed, no one doubted that he had been hexed.

Not taking his beliefs into account, Mr. Petion presented a rather typical picture of severe depression. However, convincing him that a culturally aware psychiatrist could remove the "hex" was a delicate matter—something that could be accomplished only with the help of those who not only shared Mr. Petion's beliefs, but who also believed in the power of modern medicine.

THE PHILIPPINES—MOVING ON

The Philippines could be an almost perfect example of granularity in the Pacific isles. The Philippine archipelago was the only area of Southeast Asia colonized by Europeans before it even developed either a centralized government or an elite culture. In 1571, fifty years after the arrival of the Spanish, Manila, the current capital, was founded. During the Spanish-American War (1899–1901), U.S. armed forces helped the Philippine Independence Movement, but subsequently suppressed it and took over the government. Independence, originally promised as early as 1934, became a reality in 1946; however, a continued strong United States presence exerted a potent influence for many years, during which time many Filipinos joined the U.S. armed forces and emigrated to the United States.

Today the Philippines is a country with more than 77 million inhabitants; it has an adult literacy of 95.5 percent and an urban population of almost 60 percent. Services represent 53.3 percent of the gross national product (GNP) and employ 40 percent of the population. In general, 27.9 percent of the people who emigrate from the Philippines come to their first destination: the United States. (1–3).

It is common for nursing schools in the Philippines to have courses in English that follow the standards of American schools, thus preparing their students to take nursing examinations that will permit them to work in U.S. hospitals. As a result, Filipino nurses have excelled in many hospitals in the United States. Considering the presence in the United States of relatives who have successfully emigrated, as well as a culture of successful educational progression, young people today in the Philippines are well positioned for successful long-term careers in a more advanced country. This is not very different from the emergent culture of successful engineers from schools in India, who have obtained jobs in the United States.

Ms. Estelita Brown was greatly influenced by highly educated and entrepreneurial relatives who were determined to advance beyond any obstacles; these relatives also belonged to several branches of the family that represented the very history of the country. Her father, Mr. Albert Brown, was an American soldier who had married her mother, Ms. Lourdes Dominguez, and stayed in the Philippines. Thus, he had started the Filipino branch of the Brown family, several of whose members had already emigrated to the United States before Estelita Brown had.

Ms. Brown's case presented extraordinary opportunities for those interested in cross-cultural psychiatry. If she became a nurse and was able to use her roots from the Philippines with her personal knowledge of depression and its treatment, she could be at the very front of our community efforts to educate the public about mental illness—especially in areas with high concentrations of Filipinos, where she could be easily welcome and effective.

FEELINGS AND DISEASES

Ms. Rafaela Lopez belonged to a Mexican community that paid extensive attention to death and dying. Her husband Rogelio had suffered from coronary heart disease, chronic congestive heart failure, and a slow but relentless general decline, leading to many weeks in bed followed by a protracted agony and death. All of this had been very draining and painful to the family, especially to Ms. Lopez, who had been in charge of the funeral arrangements, the masses, the nine days of praying in church, and the multiple details expected from such a loving wife. The procession to the cemetery had been especially harrowing, with almost the whole community marching after the coffin. Following the interment, there were many details regarding the care of the grave that needed attention. Ms. Lopez, always dressed totally in black, had spent many warm days at the cemetery, fussing with the flowers, the soil, the tombstone, and many other related concerns.

Once the phalanxes of friends and well-wishers had receded and her children had gone back to the United States, Ms. Lopez found herself alone. Without Rogelio as her constant companion, she was empty-handed and idle. The house appeared bigger, darker, and colder. Her friends seemed distant; her routines felt unnecessary. She became uninterested in cooking or doing the house chores; she lost weight, couldn't eat, and started wondering whether she would follow Rogelio very soon.

Ms. Lopez's neighbors alerted her children that their mother seemed to be going rapidly downhill. They couldn't come back to stay in Mazatlan, Mexico, but they could try to care for Ms. Lopez in Miami. She accepted their request that she come to Miami mostly because she thought she would rather die surrounded by her children.

Ms. Lopez, like Mr. Petion, was unaware that there could be physicians interested in her illness and its manifested symptoms. "I don't have any pain *y estoy de luto* ["and I am in mourning"] . . . the last thing I need is for somebody to come to take my blood and give me things I don't need." Ms. Lopez was quite aware that many others in her community had gone through the same ordeal she was experiencing, some of them actually dying after months of suffering. However, she didn't know of anyone who had seen a physician and had been helped. She believed that you just didn't treat the aftermath of a loss by medical means.

Feelings are primary considerations among Latinos. Sadness after a loss is seen as natural, expected, even honorable. Disease is seen either as a challenge imposed by higher powers, or as punishment. In either case, a heavy dose of fatalism and pessimism leads to late treatment or no treatment at all.

However, exceptions are becoming increasingly common, mainly among educated Latinos with a more balanced view of life. They see illness as independent from sin and believe that medicine may have the answers to some of their problems and suffering.

When a disease has been present in the same family for several generations, the family's attitude can also gradually change; it may become less emotional and more realistic about the need for medical treatment. Unfortunately, this doesn't seem to apply as easily to disorders manifested by emotional changes, which are not always considered illnesses—even when they lead to severe disability and even suicide.

LANGUAGE

We may not be able to speak of culture without measuring the influence of language. Neither one is static. Both change, sometimes together. People with the same genetic make-up may share the same language. Languages may have developed from the same roots, and may have diversified as people became different. These changes were not necessarily equivalent; while Ethiopians are genetically similar to other Africans, their language is more similar to that of Middle Easterners. (1–4).

Using a language tree as demonstration, imagine the trunk as being a proto-Indo-European great-grandfather that eventually sprouted at least nine branches—including Anatolian, Celtic, Romance, Germanic, Baltic, Slavonic, Iranian, Indic, and Greek. Theories such as the so-called "Kurgan hypothesis," use the invasion of Europe and western Asia by nomadic warriors during the early Bronze Age as the predecessor of some 144 Indo-European languages, which include English, Spanish, and all other Germanic, Roman, Slavic, Indian, and Iranian languages.

After some 6,500 years of expansion, differentiation, and enrichment of many languages, a new phenomenon has come into existence: a new linguistic order created by demographic trends, new technologies, and international communications. By the year 2050, the languages with the largest numbers of native speakers will most likely be Chinese, Hindi/Urdu, Arabic, English, and Spanish—which means added incentives to speak at least two languages. In the meantime, we need to work within today's conditions. In the southern United States for example, English is much richer in words that apply to the individual, whereas Spanish seems to have been developed for the group culture. Common English expressions, such as "He elbowed his way out," or "I felt crowded," are close to impossible to translate into Spanish. This means that the culturally competent clinician must be well-versed in the differences between English and Spanish.

THE SEVEN As*

The National Latino Behavioral Health Association (NLBHA) has adopted seven concepts that should permit the integration of cultural competence to human services. The concepts are not controversial and are often mentioned in discussions of strategies to eliminate disparities in health care. We can demonstrate these concepts using the examples of Mr. Petion, Ms. Brown, and Ms. Lopez.

Assessment: Mr. Petion was hexed, Ms. Lopez had suffered a major loss, and Ms. Brown was depressed. A culturally relevant assessment would suggest that their symptoms pointed to the same condition.

---

* Studies of programs that actually address disparities affecting Latino families share a number of characteristics. These are defined as the "7 As", following Romero's model for integrating cultural competency in human services.

Once the same diagnosis has been made, it would become clear that their needs would be different. It would be realistic to expect that Mr. Petion and Ms. Lopez would not be available for treatment unless culturally relevant interventions changed their perceptions of their problems—at least at the beginning. Since Ms. Brown has just migrated to the United States, she may find an additional and typical American problem: being uninsured, which presents a major obstacle to adequate treatment.

A complete assessment should include the evaluation of resources available to each of our potential patients according to their needs.

Administration: Here we encounter a problem that is evident to those who study the use of public facilities by ethnic minority individuals: they just do not use them. In San Diego, for example, the representation of Latinos in public programs does not correspond to their numbers in the community. Latinos just do not trust public facilities.

Instead, large numbers of Latinos go to non-governmental facilities financed by the community. If those facilities are to be used in helping address the disparities in health care and mental health care, solid and relevant representation of ethnic minorities in administration capacities will continue to be a requirement.

Availability: We try to separate availability from accessibility by thinking that the first refers to the facility itself and the second to the people who interact at the facility. If, as is often the case, the facilities are staffed, organized, scheduled, and financed along lines used for other populations, they are likely to fail those minorities who want services close to their homes, non-traditional hours, and a staff attuned to their needs, and finally, financial considerations should include the care of people who are poor, needy, and homeless.

Accessibility: This is easily the most complex concept of the "7 As". Mr. Petion and Ms. Lopez may not have access to care not because a facility is far away, but because, if offered, they are likely to reject it.

Lack of medical understanding and literacy may keep many people away from medical facilities. Further, minority populations are not necessarily friendly towards medical and technological concepts, and some, like mental disorder or depression, may be rejected outright. Thus, lack of access may exist because the person may not want the types of medical services offered at a facility. But, even if the individual does want the services, there are still many obstacles to accessibility. These include lack of relevant information, financing, transportation, culturally acceptable treatments, and effective communication with the facility's staff. Recent studies also suggest that disparities in health and mental health care may be related to the mis-distribution of health and mental health professionals. In other words, the professionals who serve the people living in poverty may in turn, not have access to the hospitals where the best health and mental health care can be obtained.*

Appropriateness: We assume that Mr. Petion, Ms. Lopez, and Ms. Brown are referred to the same facility and they have the same disorder. However, the strategies for their health care management may be quite different. Some of us recall Dr. Lawrence Kubie, the extraordinary therapist who advised that we should not dispute our patient's belief that two plus two adds to three, until we all agree that it may be four. We may not believe in Mr. Petion's hexing and may not agree that Ms. Lopez's symptoms do not need treatment. We may agree that both are suffering and both deserve all the available help. In the process, hopefully, we may reach enough mutual understanding to open the door to effective treatment. Ms. Brown's current worries relate to confidentiality, the privacy of medical records, and her future as a nurse. She needs clear and precise information about her

---

* Although the poor are known to be regular users of emergency departments, they usually do not have access to the more sophisticated services of the best centers, often because they lack access to good and reliable regular medical care. This issue is further developed in Chapter 10.

treatment and her expectations. Above all, her therapist wants her to succeed. Treatment will have been appropriate if all three receive the help they sorely need.

Affordability: Health care is costly, and many patients lack insurance or a place of entry into an adequate health care program. Ethnic minority health professionals are increasingly creating centers that bring medical care to the financial level of most patients. This continues to require much effort, patience, and perseverance. We believe that health care will be denied if ethnic minority professionals do not take the initiative to open as many doors as possible.

Accountability: Health care programs are accountable to many stakeholders. The clearer the relationship between the treatment center and the community, the more it will provide the health care services the community needs. Even when government funds are the key source of support, the community needs to participate in the allocation of resources and programs. Credibility in the community is critical to the success of any health care intervention, and it exists only when the programs respond to real community needs and concerns.

Any discussion of cultural issues in health care goes back to two major factors: *access* and *quality.* Much of our discussion in this book refers to improving access to health and mental health care and improving the quality of health and mental health services as the two key ways of eliminating disparities in health and mental health care.

TREATMENT OF MENTAL ILLNESS

Great progress has been made in understanding the distribution and treatment of psychiatric disorders. However, much more needs to be done. The World Health Organization (WHO) has used the Composite International Diagnostic Interview (CIDI) to demonstrate that psychiatric disorders are common and under-treated around the world. This fact was recently reported on a survey of 60,463 participating adults in fourteen countries in the Americas (Colombia, Mexico and United States), Europe (Belgium, France, Germany, Italy, Netherlands, Spain and Ukraine), the Middle East and Africa (Lebanon and Nigeria), and Asia (Japan and the People's Republic of China). The psychiatric disorders were classified as serious, moderate, or mild. Included was an assessment of treatment during the preceding twelve months. There was a wide variation in the response rate. The overall prevalence of psychiatric disorders also varied widely; the proportion of individuals with severe or moderate disorders was smaller than the proportion of those with mild disorders, and the proportion of respondents who received health care treatment during the twelve months before the interview varied greatly across the surveys. Though developed countries treated a larger proportion of respondents, there was a correlation between psychiatric disorders' severity and probability of treatment in every survey. Even so, a large proportion of those receiving treatment in each country either suffered from a mild disorder or a disorder that was not considered by the survey.

This report also showed that psychiatric disorders are highly prevalent, are often associated with serious impairments, and frequently go untreated. The results, however, do not throw light on strategies for better allocation of resources, better identification of candidates for health and mental health care, or better understanding of the factors that facilitate or limit treatment. Given that the information we currently have is still imperfect, those interested in cross-cultural psychiatry do best by continuing to bring the facts we now have to all of those who may have a say on the diagnosis and treatment of people with mental illness. (1–5).

TOWARDS CULTURAL COMPETENCE

The Health Resources and Services Administration of the U.S. Department of Health and Human Services has identified a pattern of characteristic practices of health care centers that promote cultural competence. (1–6). They are as follows:

1. To permanently engage with the communities being served to identify needs; to mobilize or create community resources to address those needs; and to continually reassess and redesign the delivery of services based on expressed needs.
2. To insure professional and ongoing methods of training staff and community members in both the knowledge and practices needed to develop and carry out activities, protocols, and service delivery in appropriate and culturally sensitive ways.
3. To establish cultural competence as an integral, replicable, and sustainable component of the community's health care delivery system.

The task requires that the health care program a) define culture broadly, b) value the individual's cultural beliefs; c) recognize the complexity of language interpretation; d) facilitate learning between professionals and communities; e) involve the community in defining and addressing service needs; f) collaborate with other agencies; g) professionalize staff hiring and training; and h) institutionalize cultural competence.

COMMUNITY-BASED PARTICIPATORY RESEARCH

The Centers for Disease Control and Prevention (CDC) makes a good case for community-based participatory research (CBPR), which involves a partnership between community advocates and researchers. Community leaders may be able to make differences that they do not know how to measure; and researchers may be able to measure differences they don't make.

Here are the proposed keys to success: 1) developing relationships at various levels within the community, 2) valuing diverse cultural perspectives, 3) placing equal emphasis and importance on community knowledge and academic perspectives, and 4) allowing for flexibility in research methods. All of this is of course, much more easily proposed than done.

In this respect, a beginning may be the creation of a registry that includes demographic data and also information relevant to one or several clinical problems (i.e., diabetes, depression, etc.). A second step may be a discussion with all relevant professionals about the reasons for the study and the possible outcomes. For example, in the case of diabetes among many ethnic minorities we find that the disorder is not identified, the patient is not referred, and, among those who come to the clinic, many do not follow through with the appropriate diagnostic tests and the treatment. Learning about the difference between compliant and noncompliant patients would be very useful. Also useful would be the understanding of the differences between those who accept treatment and those who reject treatment within the family.

As we approach a decision about the differences to be studied, another problem emerges: there is a gap between *measuring* differences and *making* differences. In many cases, information is available. The Diabetes Prevention Program (DPP), sponsored by the National Institute of Diabetes and Digestive and Kidney Diseases, assigned adults at high risk of developing diabetes to a nonintervention control group, a medication group (metformin), or a lifestyle intervention group with dietary and physical activity interventions. The drug reduced the rate of diabetes by about one third, while the lifestyle intervention reduced it by two-thirds. In helping the minorities, researchers may want to demonstrate the difference minority programs may make: the Connecticut Association for United Spanish Action (CAUSA) is working with Yale University in the evaluation of a recently-funded diabetes prevention program.

Two areas of trouble exist in some programs that seem to be moving towards success. Researchers need to be prepared to share control over financial resources and decisions with community representatives. They also need to be committed to a working relationship built on trust and equality. These principles need to be fully implemented if the project is to have any chance of success. (1–7).

MEDICAL LITERACY—QUALITY INDICATORS

The Institute of Medicine and the American Medical Association (1–8) have established that low health literacy is a pervasive barrier to health care. A simple test, selecting the proper spoon to administer medicine, that turns out to be very difficult for many. Very few people can pick up a spoon that holds a traditional 5 ml. of liquid. Nearly half of all American adults, or 90 million people, have difficulty understanding and using the health information that is dispensed by physician's offices and in hospital discharge instructions. When patients can't read informed consent forms, protocols for tests, discharge instructions, prescriptions, or explanations about the prescriptions, their care becomes ineffective, expensive, and frustrating to all involved.

To change this situation we must ask patients if they have any doubts or concerns; we must encourage them to bring a list of all medications to appointments; get the results of all tests; discuss with the practitioners their desire to go to the best hospital for a given procedure; and make sure they understand what will happen if they need surgery. The AMA Foundation has proposed steps that help patients understand medical instructions: 1) encourage patients to ask questions and offer them appropriate paperwork; 2) reassure them that many people have difficulty understanding health care information; 3) speak slowly and cover only two or three concepts at a time; 4) read written material aloud to patients and underline key points; 5) ask patients to paraphrase what you just explained or say "Tell me what you will do and how you will do it when you're home."; 6) suggest that patients bring a friend or relative to the counseling and planning portion of the appointment; and 7) schedule an in-service meeting with your staff to discuss low health literacy and ensure that the office is on the lookout for the related problems.

The implementation of these ideas is time consuming and often cumbersome. Managed-care companies have tried to trivialize the use of medications in psychiatry and invented the "medication check" to be completed in a few minutes. These companies have however failed to appreciate the complexities involved in these situations and circumstances.

We will use two case examples of patients to address some of these complexities: *Ms. Paula Lowe*, an African-American patient, and *Ms. María Valenzuela*, a Latina patient. Both patients were born in south San Diego. They shared many attributes: being poor and not finishing high school; being pregnant as teenagers; having large families; and having become great-grandmothers by the time we met. They both worked hard at home and in low-paying, unskilled jobs. They had also gained a great deal of weight. Mrs. Lowe developed coronary heart disease. Ms. Valenzuela developed diabetes and complications that affected her vision. Both patients have children and grandchildren incarcerated in the ever-growing California Department of Corrections. Both had to travel to prisons far from San Diego to see their relatives. Also, both were depressed and had severe disabilities as a result of depression. In their cases, we thought that effective treatment should include psychotherapy and medications. For both these women, it came as a surprise to them that their tiredness, lack of energy, inability to think or to concentrate, and pessimism might be produced by a new illness. This was a challenge because depression was added to a growing list of diagnoses, and the new treatment could add to their metabolic problems.

We thought that their belief systems, expectations, perceptions of their physicians, and comfort level at our office would determine both adherence to treatment and treatment outcome. In both cases we thought we should spend a substantial amount of time working on an adequate treatment plan. Ms. Lowe had no available relative to help us, but brought in a neighbor. Ms. Valenzuela brought in a granddaughter she had raised, a registered nurse.

We are increasingly making written material on psychiatric diagnoses and treatments, known cultural factors, psychotherapy, medications, and other pertinent materials available to our patients, their relatives, and other relevant persons, hoping to advance to a point where we are real partners in the care of each patient. Although there are many useful publications, some even translated into Spanish, we continue to lack sufficient documentation to be able to say that the information we share is adequate. As in other areas of ethnic minority care, the care of mental disorders can be greatly improved by the production and distribution of appropriate medical information.

Ms. Lowe and Ms. Valenzuela may want to know whether the health care they currently receive is the best possible. Here is where the American Psychiatric Association (APA) has been trying to help. In 1997, the APA established the Task Force on Quality Indicators. This group was charged with developing clinically-based and patient-focused quality indicators. (1–9).

In the course of its work, the task force developed a standard description for each indicator that included:

1. *Recommendation/goal*: an important clinical principle that reflects quality patient care.
2. *Indicator*: a component of quality patient care.
3. *Measure*: a mechanism or instrument to quantify the indicator.
4. *Standard*: levels of measurement that suggest that the component of health care is of adequate quality.

Access, quality, perception of care, and outcomes became the framework for discussing and selecting possible indicators:

A. Access
1. To effective medication
2. To effective psychosocial treatment
3. To appropriate specialized services

B. Quality

1. Comprehensive evaluation
2. Appropriate use of medication
3. Appropriate provision of psychosocial treatment
4. Appropriate use of screening/prevention services

C. Perceptions of Care

1. Patient
2. Family
3. Clinician

D. Outcomes

1. Improved level of functioning, improved quality of life, and minimization of social and economic cost
2. Reduction or stabilization of symptoms

Examples:

A. Access

1. Access to new antipsychotics for patients with schizophrenia
2. Availability of ECT for patients for whom it is indicated
3. Children and adolescents should have access to appropriate evaluation and treatment services

B. Quality

1. Current treatment with an antidepressant medications for patients with major depressive disorder irrespective of the severity of the illness
2. Screening of patients for substance abuse disorders
3. Appropriate use of psychosocial treatments for a severe and persistently mentally ill (SPMI) population

C. Perceptions of Care

1. Assessment of patient's perception of care
2. Assessment of families' perception of care
3. Assessment of clinician's perception of care

D. Outcomes
> 1. Resumption of productive activities by patients with severe and persistent mental illness when no longer in the acute phase of the illness
> 2. Stabilization of the patient's weight in every new *DSM-IV* diagnosis of anorexia nervosa

The APA Task Force on Quality Indicators saw the development of quality indicators as a work in progress. As we better understand the most important factors in the practice of psychiatry, we will develop a better understanding of the indicators that apply to settings, diagnoses, treatments, and outcomes. For instance, take the cases of Ms. Valenzuela and Ms. Lowe. Which factors will lead to a better diagnosis? The clinician will certainly need to understand their perception of their illnesses, their preconceptions about therapies offered to them, and their misgivings about long-term use of medications. If either one was deemed to be non-responding, other indicators will emerge: Can she afford the medication? Is she adhering to her medication regimen? When should the medication be evaluated again if she is not responding? Is she suicidal? Is the home environment a factor in maintaining the depression? In what way would other settings be of benefit for the patient?

Indicators of quality of treatment before, during, and after hospitalization are increasingly important. Quality of care at the time of hospital discharge includes a number of matters: Is the patient not suicidal? Is the family properly informed of her present condition? Whom is she going to live with? Who will provide supervision? Who will provide transportation for follow-up appointments? Does she realistically have access to medications? Does she really have access to the place where follow-up appointments will take place? What is relevant in further planning?

We take the position that the development of quality indicators is as important as, or more important than the creation of clinical instruments, protocols, and rules that may not be followed. Quality indicators permit a cross-sectional view of the treatment in progress and a more practical approach to emerging problems that are often complex and difficult. We envision the use of quality indicators as one of the best ways to improve the level and quality of health care and to eliminate disparities. This is so because we can develop indicators that apply to populations with specific problems or with cultural characteristics that might require special clinical attention.

We have treated Ms. Lowe and Ms. Valenzuela for many years now. Ms. Lowe has lost weight, has had a steady medical progress, takes fewer medications, and has learned to influence some of her family members who are ready to listen to her, and wait for others who are following their own paths. Ms. Valenzuela struggles less with her weight and her diabetes, has had no new complications, is less depressed, and has learned that she has more control over her life than she had previously anticipated, even though that control is difficult to use as steadily as she might want.

As we advance in the presentation of clinical facts, situations, and developments relevant to a better cultural understanding of our patients, we will again and again promote quality indicators. An ideal situation is one in which new relevant knowledge leads to the development of indicators that, like traffic signals, permit a better negotiation of difficult situations along our clinical road.

CHAPTER TWO

TONES OF BLUE
Major Depression

Mabruka

Mabruka saw her family destroyed, sometimes a person at a time, in the numerous armed upheavals that destroyed most of her country in Northern Africa during her childhood and for a number of years thereafter. A long time later she told us she had come to believe that people lived for short times, disappeared suddenly, and nobody could count on being alive from one day to the next.

Mabruka had not yet learned how to smile when we met her at the age of 28 years. She said she didn't remember not feeling sad. At any time she would suffer several symptoms of depression, and they would often be accompanied by respiratory symptoms suggestive of an anxiety disorder. She recalled that at different times she had been seen by nurses working with relief teams that told her the symptoms were because she was anemic and suffered asthma.

Mabruka came to the United States as a refugee sponsored by a religious group. Her first years in America were not easy. She felt isolated, different from others and with no clear direction as to where her life might go. Her main social outlet was the church that had sponsored her. Many of its members took a liking to Mabruka, and as she started visiting their homes, several people started working on getting her an education and providing a job. Young and increasingly strong, Mabruka proved to be an excellent worker at a warehouse, where she seemed not to mind any kind of job, including lifting boxes, mopping, painting and loading trucks.

A lady at her church who was active with NAMI recognized in her the same symptoms she had seen among people suffering depression and anxiety. She recommended the evaluation that led us to meeting Mabruka, a shy and self-effacing young woman whose voice was very soft. She was always pleasant and willing to listen to our ideas about her diagnosis and treatment.

Mabruka was not familiar with the concepts of depression and anxiety. She had always felt her symptoms were produced by something wrong with her blood, her metabolism or her lungs. She was initially reluctant to believe that she met the criteria for two psychiatric disorders and that psychiatrists could help her feel healthier than ever before.

Antidepressants and interpersonal psychotherapy most likely helped Mabruka adapt to her new life, hold a steady job, move to a nicer place, start to study to take the General Education Diploma (GED), and take driving lessons while trying to save money to buy a car.

Mabruka not only learned to smile, she started to dress better, to take much better care of her appearance, and to seek new social contacts. She even obtained help from several international organizations to try to locate the surviving members of her family, and start communicating with them.

This is one of many patients that have taught us that chronic, unremitting depression seemingly destined to accompany the person forever, responds to treatment. These patients often come from places where there is no access to psychiatrists, there is no great public interest in mental health, and the symptoms of depression or anxiety are attributed to organic conditions. Given these circumstances, it is no mystery that our interventions are not sought, may not be appreciated, or may not be continued long enough to obtain sustained benefits.

Before we undertake a healing process for many minority patients, we have to understand the additional problems they face. Victor Villaseñor grew up in California (Note 2-1). Though he started his life in a nurturing place where Spanish was spoken and a loving family surrounded him, his world was shattered the first day of school when he found Latinos were not welcome. His family was no longer the same: "My mother, who I'd always thought was so beautiful, I could clearly see she wasn't. Her brown skin was the color of dirt and her dark eyes were too large, and her hair was black and her lips were too big. . . ."

Victor was suddenly seeing his family through eyes that were not his. As an adult and as an acclaimed writer, Victor could later explain how racism works.

Mabruka went through similar experiences when she came to understand that she was going to live in a world in which her appearance, her way of speaking, and her ways of behaving made her different from others, and the others were the immense majority. Her minimal self-esteem seemed to disappear, and she began to think that not only the outside world was very difficult, but that she was internally flawed. It took her a very long time to understand that she was not what others thought or may think of her, and that she could create a world much more attractive to her, in which she was unique and no less than others.

Mabruka was in for a new surprise when, as an Ethiopian, she thought she was the prototypical African American. She learned that she belonged to yet another minority: those in the first generation of migrants from Africa destined to build their own place in America. With time she learned that her attitude, her hard work and her desire to succeed carved a unique place for her in the midst of many others of very different origins.

Karen and Abram

Karen told us she had never known her original name. For that matter, she never knew anyone in her family of origin. Her physical appearance agreed with the opinion of the nuns at the orphanage in Vietnam where she grew up: She most likely was the daughter of an African-American soldier and a girl from Saigon. An American couple adopted her when she was twelve years of age, when she suddenly found herself with parents, grandparents, uncles, aunts, siblings, and pets. She was not the person in the family who was depressed. It was her very responsible, punctilious, rigid, adoptive father who could no longer survive his own pangs of conscience about not being good enough.

Abram, the father, had belonged to a Christian family in Iran. His father had been a successful engineer during the Shah's long administration, and had been careful to bring his family and his fortune to the United States years before the revolution. Abram was the second oldest child. He became very anxious and obsessed with details in his early teens. By then his older sister had gotten married just after finishing high school, became part of her husband's large family, and gradually left her own siblings and her background behind her. At the time of the sister's wedding, the parents entered a noisy, bitter and long divorce proceeding. While the parents fought, Abram was left in charge of three younger siblings. His anxiety increased, he became more uncertain of himself, and became even more worried about details and events at home. It was then when he started checking doors, shelves, and other places in the house, trying to make sure everything was fine.

Abram went away to college, leaving his younger siblings with the mother. He later remembered his four years in college as the best of his life. His symptoms practically disappeared. He dated a classmate, an easy-going, down-to-earth, understanding girl, whom he married shortly after graduating *magna cum laude*. He received many job offers, one of the best of them in the United States.

Abram's symptoms gradually came back after his first two children were born; he took more responsibilities, and started worrying about his contributions to society. It was his wife's idea to adopt a child who was unlikely to be helped by any one else. This was the reason why they went through the long and arduous process of adopting the Vietnamese girl who eventually became Karen.

Karen seemed to immediately adapt to the family, was a major help from the beginning, showed great talent for mathematics, and soon became her father's informal assistant. While Karen was still a teenager, Abram came to us and described the multiple symptoms that had been with him intermittently since his early teens, his multiple doubts and concerns, and his more recent inability to cope, his insomnia, his lack of energy, his lack of ability to think or to concentrate, and his increasingly frequent ideas of death. A central theme of the illness was that he didn't deserve his family, and his wife should divorce him. He had changed this idea into the certainty that his wife was actually going to divorce him, and the children would go through the same distress he experienced as a teenager. In his thoughts about the future, he saw a re-orphaned and fully Americanized Karen going back to Vietnam.

As is the case with some 80 percent of the patients we treat with psychotherapy and antidepressant medications, Abram responded well to treatment. His wife was very supportive, and the children, including Karen, helped greatly in the long process of separating illness from fact, and showing Abram that depression creates thoughts and feelings that are not backed by real experiences.

Teresa

Karen's supportive attitude and very positive feelings towards her family reminded us of those of Teresa, who became our patient, even though she requested help for her mother and not for herself. By the time of our first interview, the mother had been suffering for several years a progressive decline in her brain functions as a result of repeated big and small strokes she had experienced over the course of several years. The mother was paralyzed on one side, could hardly utter any words, was disoriented, and could barely assist Teresa in bringing her in to the office by wheelchair.

As often happens in a family with several children, Teresa's siblings had gradually delegated care of the mother to her, so that Teresa went from coordinating the mother's support to eventually being the only caregiver. Without realizing it, Teresa moved, step-by-step, from having a life of her own, to using all her spare time for the mother's care. Teresa abandoned her apartment and moved to a house where she could organize a mini hospital for the mother. She could work as a successful banker only because she had a person covering for her at home during the day, and, even so, would call home many times a day to make sure her instructions were followed.

Teresa trained herself to identify every change in her mother's attitude, facial expression and movements as indicative of the mother's wishes, interests and thoughts. Teresa decided to prepare all the meals herself, and tried to provide all the nursing care the mother could need.

During our first conversation with Teresa, we learned she was the last of five children born to one of the many Chinese families in Baja California, Mexico. The family had never abandoned the family traditions, so that the children expected to provide support and care to their parents for life. As the older children, all capable and ambitious, obtained a higher education and excellent jobs elsewhere in the United States, Teresa stayed home, and got her education locally. Though all the siblings came to the assistance of the mother, especially after the father died, each of them found that outside commitments would keep them far away.

Our conversations about providing more skillful care to the mother in a proper facility led to discussing Teresa's life and current situation. She was despondent, and saw her life as static and with little future. She slept poorly, her performance at work had considerably deteriorated, she felt very guilty about her constant frustration with her mother, and bitter at being abandoned by her siblings. She often felt that she would be better off dead.

The process of talking Teresa into letting go of her mother led to learning about the many obligations she had, because of her heritage and her family values, and also because of the assumption that only within the family could the mother possibly receive adequate care. It was easy to point out to her that she might not live long the way she was going, and that accepting new alternatives might enhance her opportunities and her mother's survival chances. Teresa eventually accepted psychotherapy and antidepressant medication for herself.

Samporn and Pablo

Samporn had been an example of health, productivity, vigor and enthusiasm, both before and after migrating to the United States from Cambodia. He had always had the feeling that he could sell anything. In San Diego, he went into business with a cousin who had immigrated several years earlier, and had a successful auto repair shop. With his first savings, Samporn bought an old car, worked on it diligently, and sold it well, making a substantial profit. After repeating the operation a number of times, Samporn started his own used car business: he would go around selecting old and dilapidated cars that he would repair and sell. He improved the business when he changed strategies: he would talk to the potential customer, get an idea of the year and the car make wanted, find a car as approximate as possible, calculate the costs of improving it, add these costs and his commission, sell the car before repairing it, and offer a six-month guarantee.

Samporn was going at full speed when he started to experience a dull pain beneath his ribs. It would increase and decrease, but seemed to be always there. His appetite decreased, and he started to lose considerable weight. Then he developed abdominal discomfort and bloating. After tests, much to his surprise, at the age of 44 years,

Samporn heard from his physician that he had cancer of the stomach, and needed to have an immediate gastrectomy. The surgery was successful. Samporn now was free from cancer, but not well at all. He couldn't sleep, couldn't eat, continued to lose weight, couldn't work because of lack of energy, initiative and interest, and started to appear worse than before the surgery. The surgeon recommended a psychiatric consultation that led to the diagnosis of and eventual treatment of a major depression.

Pablo was born without a problem in his life. The youngest of eleven children, he grew up in the midst of more than two hundred relatives, which meant that he had an invitation to a large party almost every weekend. After high school, he joined an uncle's bakery, which he saw as the perfect opportunity to enjoy frequent treats. In a family of overweight people, Pablo showed early that he was destined to be the heaviest. Warnings about diabetes, hardening of the arteries, high blood pressure, and related dreadful problems fell on deaf ears, mostly because the warnings seemed to be direct challenges to Pablo's perception of the way he wanted to live his life.

There was consternation in the family when jovial, nice, friendly, easygoing forty-two year-old Pablo was rushed to the hospital after suffering a convulsion. During the acute treatment period, the family seemed to hear "hyper" constantly: hypertension, hyperglycemia, hypercholesterolemia, and in their ears, many more "hypers," all of which sounded pretty dreadful.

Pablo was devastated when he came out of the hospital. Not only had he been told that he had serious medical problems, he had also been told that he needed to change his ways if he wanted to survive. His distress and concerns were translated into more eating "to calm my nerves," and minimal compliance with his medication. He became morose, much less interested in his work, less gregarious, less involved in family affairs, much less visible in places where he had been very popular, and progressively more oblivious of others. When he started to neglect his physical appearance, there was a meeting of concerned relatives who requested that he visit the family physician. Pablo was then referred to a psychiatrist for treatment of depression.

The very process of getting Pablo to the psychiatrist was as difficult as bringing him to the hospital when he had the convulsion. He finally agreed to make the first visit as a favor to his parents, but not necessarily because he thought anything good could come out of it. He was surprised to learn that the psychiatrist had a medical degree, was quite interested in his metabolic problems, and was willing to work with him in getting him out of his current predicaments. Pablo's interpretation of all of this was that he had found a friend who understood him, understood his feelings and fears, and perhaps could help him find a way to develop a new lifestyle that might be acceptable. The relationship developed into an alliance that eventually permitted the creation of an effective strategy for treatment.

Papa Chen

Papa Chen had been one of the most popular persons in the barrio. His grocery store had preceded the Latinos, so that everybody had business with Mr. Chen, often starting as children. Every one seemed to have an expense account at the store, and Mr. Chen seemed to sell every day of the month and be paid once a month. The barrio and the store had grown together, so that Mr. Chen had expanded the business to sell Mexican clothing, cowboy boots, piñatas, tortillas, and, more recently, reading glasses and canes, besides numerous items that Mr. Chen brought to the store at the request of the customers. The store doubled or tripled as community center and gathering place for many.

Word in the barrio was that Mr. Chen spoke more Spanish than English, though that was difficult to know because Mr. Chen communicated mostly by gestures and treats, so that every kid knew that Mr. Chen kept all sorts of candy and cookies for kids frequenting the store.

One day, Mrs. Chen, for the first time since anyone remembered, was alone at the store. As she was the next day and many more days. Her only answer to questions about Mr. Chen was "Away." After a couple of weeks, she was often in tears, seemed to be absent, and acted as if she had lost all interest in the store. The local diocese provided a Korean priest who came to talk to her. She finally opened up and revealed that her husband was in bed dying. Both she and her husband considered his death imminent. For several months he had lost sleep and energy, had lost his appetite, and had finally taken to bed. They saw the situation as hopeless, so had not even considered a medical examination. With help from the priest and much prodding from Mr. Chen's many friends, an evaluation at the local clinic was arranged. He was found to be underweight, undernourished, and dehydrated. He was transferred to the hospital. A Korean resident in psychiatry was summoned to help in translation. He did much more than that: he presented a convincing case that Mr. Chen was suffering a major depression and urgently needed psychiatric treatment.

Recovery was quite slow, but a few months later, a day when the store was full of people, when there were more smiles, hugs, and congratulations than ever before in the same place, Mr. Chen reemerged behind the counter, again strong and again offering friendly gestures and friendlier treats to the children.

DEPRESSION? WHAT'S THAT?

Many of our patients with depression do not relate their symptoms to the functioning of the brain or to a disorder that is not completely organic. For that matter, it is much easier for them to attribute the symptoms to other causes: Mabruka had led a tough life, Abram faced concerns that were very real to him, Samporn and Pablo had suffered life-threatening conditions, Teresa was overwhelmed, Papa Chen was old and seemed to have a serious physical illness. These situations are not exceptional. What would be surprising would be that a patient should think of depression immediately after the symptoms emerge. This happens, but it is usually because the person has suffered previous episodes of depression, has witnessed a depression in relatives or other people close to her, or has been exposed to the growing public information on depression.

Two other problems frequently seen among minority patients prevent the diagnosis:

Prejudice. Emotional disorders are seen as worse, more humiliating, or more embarrassing than almost any other condition. We have heard at our office statements that reveal the situation: "I never thought I would ever see a psychiatrist." "I am sure my wife was wrong when she insisted that I come to see you. I am just unable to sleep and feel distracted by the desire to cry."

Fear of discrimination. This fear is very real, and often based on facts. Some acquaintances may act as if the person brought the illness on, doesn't have the courage or the strength to handle problems on her own, or wants the symptoms as an explanation for matters that are very simple. The fact is depression is very common, can be lethal, can be treated, and the outcome in most properly treated cases is excellent.

How common? Some believe that depression affects, in one way or the other, at least half of the households in the United States. The World Health Organization estimates that by the year 2020, depression will be the second most important cause of disability in the world.

How lethal? Fifteen percent of the people who suffer depressions commit suicide. This is a staggering finding that needs change through community awareness, support for the depressed, and understanding that depression is not a personal but a community problem. Those who helped the patients we have presented here were prepared to understand that to help others is help to ourselves.

THE SYMPTOMS OF DEPRESSION (*DSM-IV-R*)

We see *depression* as a low emotional tone accompanied by physical and emotional symptoms. The four *physical symptoms* are significant change in weight and appetite, changes in sleep, agitation or retardation, and loss of energy. The four *emotional symptoms* are diminished interest or pleasure; diminished ability to think or concentrate; feelings of worthlessness or excessive or inappropriate guilt; and recurrent thoughts of death, or recurrent suicidal ideation, that is, plans or attempts to commit suicide.

Can depression be treated? Scientifically controlled studies show that antidepressants and psychotherapy are very effective and much more so when they are used together.

What are the outcomes? Most depressed patients do much better after effective treatment. Within two years, up to 80 percent of depressed patients show substantial improvement, which is more than we can say about success in treating many medical problems.

THE MOOD OF DEPRESSION IN MINORITIES

Many depressed patients complain about sadness, pessimism, hopelessness, and similar moods that suggest a low affective tone and a lack of hope in the future. Many minority patients do not have the same complaints when they have depression. As a matter of fact, they may not even relate to the word "depression." They are more likely to complain about pain (headache, abdominal pain, back pain, pain in the extremities), other somatic symptoms (dizziness, shortness of breath) or feelings of anxiety, fear of unknown dangers, boredom, discomfort, or just "not feeling well." They will often indicate that they are not "sad." The majority may accept the idea that they were suffering a depression immediately after they start to feel better.

Physical Symptoms

Many minority patients who disavow "feelings of depression" have no difficulty identifying in themselves the usual physical manifestations of depression:

- Significant weight loss when not dieting or weight gain (e.g. a change of more than 5% of body weight in a month), or decrease or increase in appetite nearly every day. Pablo, for example, had an increase in appetite when he became depressed.
- Insomnia or hypersomnia (increased sleep) nearly every day.
- Psychomotor agitation or retardation nearly every day. This manifestation is one that is easily observed by others.
- Fatigue or loss of energy nearly every day.

Emotional Symptoms

- Markedly diminished interest or pleasure. Both patients and others report that the patient no longer cares about activities that were dear to her or in which she took great pleasure.
- Feelings of worthlessness or excessive or inappropriate guilt nearly every day.
- Diminished ability to think or to concentrate, or indecisiveness, nearly every day.
- Recurrent thoughts of death, recurrent suicidal ideation, a specific plan for committing suicide, or a suicide attempt.

In order to be counted as positive, the symptoms must cause clinically significant distress or impairment in social, occupational, or other important areas of functioning. They must not be due to the direct physiological effect of a substance or a general medical condition.

DEPRESSION AND PAIN

Depressed patients have often suffered chronic pain before they go into treatment for depression. When they describe their symptoms, pain is often the first symptom they complain about. When they have a partial response to treatment, pain is one of the most prominent remaining symptoms. When they have a recurrence, they often report that their pain never went away. We believe it impossible to think of depression without thinking of pain, and hope that the knowledge of neurotransmitters associated both with pain and depression leads to more effective therapeutic responses.

SOME CLINICAL OBSTACLES TO ADEQUATE DIAGNOSIS

Depression is often difficult to diagnose. Here are some of the reasons:

The patient, as in the case of Mabruka, may have been depressed before suffering a major depression (double depression), so that the more serious symptoms may be attributed to a continuation of the older, milder disorder, which could prevent more vigorous treatment.

The patient may have suffered symptoms leading to the diagnosis of a different disorder before the depression became clear. Abram, for example, had a long history of obsessive and compulsive symptoms.

Samporn and Pablo suffered major depressions following serious physical illnesses. It is possible that the symptoms could have been attributed to their medical diagnoses. We take the position that the depressive syndrome should be treated every time it is present, regardless of other medical problems the patient may have.

Depression in old age tends to be justified by external circumstances. In the case of Papa Chen, it took an astute psychiatric resident to recognize that no matter Papa Chen's physical condition and possible external stresses, the primary diagnosis was major depression.

WHO GOES TO PSYCHIATRISTS?

Among the many people who suffer major depressions, only a small minority ever see a psychiatrist. Surveys show that potential patients are not identified, are not referred, and if given an appointment, they may not keep it.

Minority patients are among the populations known for the lowest use of psychiatric services. All the factors that contribute to not getting treatment apply to minorities: Not only are they subjected to more prejudice and more discrimination, but they may also lack knowledge about mental disorders, lack of knowledge about services available, and may also fear being diagnosed with a chronic and deteriorating mental illness. To this we should add that many have a fear of psychiatric facilities.

Most minority patients will pay more attention to the physical than to the emotional symptoms of depression. Patients may actually justify the emotional symptoms on the basis of the physical ones: They have lost interest, have difficulty thinking, feel guilty and may want to die because they feel tired and weak, can't sleep or eat, and can't even move.

Our studies in the waiting rooms of primary medical clinics (Note 2–2) show that depression is sometimes not diagnosed even when the patient in the waiting room is complaining about depression, looks depressed, and is talking about killing himself. Some primary care physicians do not refer patients to psychiatrists even when interested in doing so; fearful that the only result will be that they lose the patient to treatment.

What about people and factors that bring patients to the psychiatrists? The "Friends and Supporters of Psychotherapy" were the subject of an interesting book published in 1969. Social scientists at Columbia University showed that a friendly group accounted for a large number of referrals for psychiatric treatment (Note 2–2)

Developments in recent decades, including the emergence and empowerment of advocacy groups, the emergence of community psychiatry, the increasing recognition that disparities in health sometimes are man-made, and the increasing formation of partnerships between psychiatrists and patients, have promoted the creation of an informal "Friends and Supporters of Psychiatry." Who are they?

Former patients, their relatives, their friends, and their advocates who, together with organized psychiatry, seek ways of improving the diagnosis and treatment of psychiatric disorders.

The Friends and Supporters of Psychiatry joined us in the trenches when managed-care companies tried to eradicate psychiatric treatment. The managed-care companies enforced the role of the primary-care physician as the gatekeeper, tried to keep most patients away from mental health professionals, insisted that psychiatrists shouldn't practice psychotherapy, and tried to reduce the role of psychiatrists to just checking on medications prescribed by others. Outside of managed care companies, new coalitions of primary care physicians and psychiatrists are breaking out of the managed care restrictions, and opening new doors for better communications and meaningful interactions.

Advocates and mental health professionals went to the legislators, to Congress, to the federal government, and to the courts in order to turn back those who would destroy quality in psychiatric care. Some of our first victories were in the court of public opinion. The first victory in the U.S. Senate happened when three courageous senators stood up to describe the havoc that had been created in their own lives because of the mental illness of close relatives.

The battles with managed care clearly showed psychiatrists that friends and supporters of psychiatry represented psychiatry well because they were representing themselves.

While we psychiatrists will continue to work with federal and state legislators and regulators, with advocacy groups, and with organized medicine, those of us interested in minorities have to create forces within the community that give a voice to the mentally ill. Among Latinos, a major ally has been the *promotoras*—natural barrio leaders who have lent a loud voice to our patients who do not talk for themselves. The *promotoras* go into the community to spread the word about the frequency and severity of mental illness, the availability and the results of treatment, and the need for each person to take care of his or her own health.

Fighting the battle within the community is just the beginning. Most patients suffering depression are referred to primary-care physicians. As of this writing in 2006, based on the best evidence available to us, it is our opinion that many primary-care physicians are undertrained to deal with anything more than basic psychiatric disorders, are often underpaid by insurance companies and health maintenance organizations when they try to deal with psychiatric disorders, and may lack the knowledge to make informed decisions about referral to psychiatrists. It would hardly be an exaggeration if we claimed that the seemingly obligatory pass by primary care for many patients who should be diagnosed and treated for mental disorders is a very mixed blessing. On the other hand, psychiatrists are ready to work with primary-care physicians, and offer the following proposals:

- Directors of training in family practice, internal medicine, pediatrics, and gynecology/obstetrics should be prepared to offer solid training in depression and suicide.
- Those primary-care physicians willing to treat depression should be aware of the extent of their knowledge, their limitations, and their opportunities for interaction with psychiatrists.
- Psychiatrists should be prepared to interact with primary-care physicians, create diagnoses and treatment teams, and recognize expertise anywhere it emerges.
- Psychiatrists should be prepared to create centers of excellence that will actively interact with primary-care physicians and other colleagues interested in the best care for our patients.

CHAPTER THREE

TONES OF INDIGO
Other Depressions

Josephine

We first saw Josephine resplendent in her colorful uniform, with multiple ribbons that represented numerous achievements and recognition of her deeds in many parts of the world. She told us that her life had been the history of many lows and many highs. She grew up in a Latino military family, with her father usually absent, and her mother always trying to adjust to a new home, or getting ready to move once more. Her main source of satisfaction during her early years was being at home with her mother and her older siblings. They frequently shared stories of the gallantry of the family warriors going back to World War II.

Josephine vividly described her enormous fear and sense of loss when she first went to school. "I had a typical school phobia", she said. Her mother became a fixture in the classroom for months, withdrawing her presence from school very slowly. This situation was repeated in three different schools, in several towns and on two continents. Josephine thought she had no attachments other than to her family; no regular friends, and only a few memories that she could share for long with any group of friends.

At age twelve, Josephine was referred to a mental health professional. The report described her as a very fearful child who trusted very few people and was very insecure. The recommendation for therapy couldn't be carried out because the family moved again. In her new town, she made it as far as the waiting list in a mental health clinic. By then, Josephine's grades were quite good; she was starting to like school, and had come to think that she should follow in her great grandfather's, grandfather's and father's steps. She clearly stated: "Haven't I belonged to the army all my life? Why not make it official?" Josephine enlisted in the armed forces at seventeen, immediately after finishing high school. She was correct in thinking that not much would surprise her in the army. In due time, she went to college, decided to have a career in mechanical engineering, was commissioned after obtaining a bachelor of science degree, and was later allowed to go for a master's and a doctorate (Ph.D.) degree. Much to her surprise, she fell in love and married one of her professors; a fully committed nonmilitary philosopher who was more than glad to carry the heavy weight in raising their three daughters. One of Josephine's main distresses as an adult was to see an older brother become an alcoholic and die from cirrhosis of the liver.

Josephine was a colonel in the army when we met her. By then, she was already an expert on major depression, having had three severe episodes. Each had lasted for several months, and each was also treated successfully with the same antidepressant. After the third episode, lithium was added to her treatment. The first and second episodes of depression had followed the birth of her two younger daughters. The third episode coincided with the protracted illness and death of her mother; a very nurturing lady who, together with her large Latino family, had provided her with strong support for many years; mostly at a distance, and mostly through long letters.

In our first visit, it became clear that Josephine did not come to talk about herself. Her oldest daughter Karen was a freshman at a prestigious university in the East. At the end of the first semester, she started to call home daily, with messages that became increasingly bizarre, and suggested that she had established contact with extra-terrestrial forces and their allies on earth. Her roommate reported that she was not sleeping well, seemed to be almost always on the go, and appeared to have stopped studying altogether. Josephine wanted to make sure we would see her daughter if she were brought to our town. As Josephine was getting ready to bring her daughter home, her daughter's symptoms became worse, and had to be admitted to the University Hospital after taking more than 100 tablets of aspirin. At the hospital, the psychiatric consultant diagnosed a bipolar disorder, and started her on lithium. Her response was very rapid, and her symptoms abated within a period of days. She was discharged to her mother, who in turn brought her to our mental health clinic at a time when she appeared to be stabilized.

Immediately after discharge, Josephine's daughter decided not to fill her prescription for lithium. She explained her recent history as the result of a major misunderstanding. She had been tired; might not have slept much; and might have misinterpreted a few events around her. However, she felt that she was as fit as ever, ready to return to school, and she came home just to please her parents. It was then that we met the father, Joe; a number of years older than Josephine, wearing a beard and a beret, and reading a large book in our waiting room. Joe expressed his concern that Karen would get worse. He joined in the effort to get her to take lithium, and took her home with the promise of keeping us posted about her symptoms.

In the following days, Karen became hyperactive and talkative, and Joe proposed that she take lithium or go to the hospital. She opted for the first option, and gradually settled down over a period of a few days. She then decided to stay in town, take the semester off, go to work, and enroll in the local university after she was fully settled. Karen met her goals, went back to school, and eventually completed college. We still occasionally see her and enjoy her success. She is on her way to a key position in the local school of social work.

Another daughter of Josephine, Mollie, became depressed while in high school, requested psychiatric care, and came to our mental health clinic during the first weeks of her depression. She mentioned that Josephine had been quite supportive and interested in making sure that she received early treatment. Mollie responded to the same antidepressant as her mother. One day several years later, the third daughter of Josephine, Laurie, came to the office. She was worried about mood swings that were becoming more severe. She would experience long periods of depression, alternating with short periods of irritability and restlessness. She wanted to try lithium, which she did successfully. In many ways, Karen, Laurie, and Mollie have been successful in numerous endeavors, leading busy social lives, participating in a number of community activities, and advancing towards very fulfilling lives. They all have now taken lithium or antidepressant medication for several years. When we discussed this situation with Josephine, she commented that she was certain that early treatment had spared her three daughters from years of pain.

Kent

As described by Kent, an immigrant from Morocco, his life had changed the day he discovered an extraordinary affinity between hoses and snakes. Their shapes were generally the same, they moved in the same fashion, they were both organic, and they were both in the garden. They, however, had different kinds of lives: while hoses did not reproduce (well, not quite: hoses could be cut into little hoses) and were moved by people, snakes produced baby snakes and moved by themselves (most of the time). As Ken studied the subject, he started to spend long periods in the library where he made a discovery critical to his new theories: hoses were made of organic substances left long ago by dinosaurs, which in turn were descendants of primitive snakes. This was a direct relationship that further proved that he was dealing with a relatively homogeneous population of hoses and snakes.

Kent's sister, Jazmin, also a migrant from Morocco, first noticed the changes in Kent when he began to spend long periods at the library reading about biology, archeology, hydrocarbons, and reptiles. She was baffled when her normally coherent and logical brother started to explain to her his new theories. By then, he was eating poorly, sleeping barely two or three hours at night, and filling a number of notebooks with abundant information obtained from his readings at the library. When Jazmin finally read some of her brother's writings, she was taken aback by their apparent incoherence. Kent and Jazmin lived in a closely knit community of North African college students, most of whom had noticed Kent's absence from their circle. Jazmin enlisted their help in inquiring about Kent's sudden changes. The expected friendly exchange with Kent never took place. When his friends expressed their doubts about his new theory, Kent, in ways totally contrary to his usually easy demeanor, accused them of envy, mediocre thinking, and lack of ability to understand science.

As Kent withdrew even more into his readings and his writing, he dropped out of school and lost contact with his friends. Jazmin found herself as the only remaining contact with Kent, who became increasingly reclusive. One morning Jazmin found Kent unconscious on the floor. He had cut his wrist and was bleeding profusely. Kent was brought to the hospital, treated for his wounds, and admitted as a danger to himself. A psychiatric evaluation rendered the diagnosis of major depression with psychosis. Kent responded very well to psychotherapy and antipsychotic medications, and he was discharged after a stay of five days.

Kent subsequently refused to attend a psychiatric clinic, claiming that the medications were poisoning him, that he was perfectly well, and that his hospital stay had been unnecessary. Otherwise, he seemed to be improved. He stopped talking about snakes or hoses, went back to school, and seemed closer to the person everyone knew—however, not completely. He seemed to have lost interest in his friends, was spending much more time alone in his room, and often appeared to be daydreaming. One day, Jazmin became very upset when she came to Kent's room, and again found books about dinosaurs, hydrocarbons, hoses, and snakes. In the following weeks,

Kent got progressively worse, left school, gradually began to neglect himself, lost weight, and seemed to be sleeping minimally. Jazmin and her friends found that they couldn't do much as long as Kent refused help, but did not attempt to hurt himself. An unexpected break came when Kent, unshaved, dirty, with his hair uncombed and his clothes in disarray, showed up at the library to continue his research. When a security guard requested full identification from him, Kent became abusive, the police were called and Kent was detained. Jazmin was called, and she was instrumental in readmitting Kent to the hospital where he had been treated before.

Kent seemed to improve more slowly this time. He again received the diagnosis of major depression with psychosis. His treatment included psychotherapy, antipsychotics, and antidepressants. After several weeks in the hospital, Kent no longer entertained his bizarre ideas. He still was distant, seemingly uninterested in others. Jazmin consulted with her parents, and they decided to come to the United States to try to help their son. Kent greeted the imminent arrival of his parents with manifestations of great enthusiasm. He improved his appearance, started to show interest in all therapeutic activities, and announced that this time he was much better, was now insightful about his illness, and would fully cooperate with his treatment plans.

The meeting with his parents was highly emotional. After everyone (but Kent) finished shedding tears, Kent requested to be discharged the same day "to go and enjoy (his) parents after such a long absence." Every member of the staff was skeptical about Kent's rapid progress, and the unanimous vote was for a longer hospital stay. His parents saw Kent as a normal person who deserved a chance to be with his family. They rejected the pleas for a longer hospital stay. At the end, Kent was discharged against medical advice, in the custody of his parents, who gladly signed all the necessary documents and took him home.

Much before his first clinic appointment, and three days after he was allowed to leave the hospital, Kent hanged himself in the hotel room where his parents were staying. A very short suicide note indicated that nobody was at fault, and he was getting the freedom he always wanted.

THE MANY FACES OF DEPRESSION

Mabruka and Josephine suffered depressions preceded by long histories of anxiety symptoms. This is fairly common. In many psychiatrists' practices, half of the patients with depression have a history of anxiety, and half of the patients with anxiety also have a history of depression. Together, anxiety and depression account for half of their patients.

A panic attack, with multiple cardio-respiratory symptoms, such as shortness of breath, palpitations, chest pain, a choking sensation, and feelings of impending doom, is the most typical manifestation of an anxiety disorder. There are also patients who suffer phobias characterized by fears either localized or generalized, who may not suffer panic attacks. In obsessive-compulsive disorders, anxiety is often prominent, and the repetitive and unwelcome thoughts and actions at times appear as failed efforts at controlling anxiety. Many patients with obsessive-compulsive thinking and behavior also develop episodes of clinical depression.

Stress and post-traumatic stress disorders are also often accompanied by manifestations of anxiety and depression. The symptoms of patients who first manifest stress or post-traumatic stress disorders and evolve into a chronic course, are often difficult to separate from patients who suffer from chronic depression, which brings us to Edna.

In our opinion, Edna had a typical panic disorder, and the course of her illness was quite different from the ones shown by Mabruka or Josephine. Edna's concern had always been her heart. In her late teens, she underwent numerous studies to rule out organic pathology related to shortness of breath and palpitations. In her twenties and thirties, she often went by ambulance to the hospital because of the same symptoms. In her late thirties, she finally saw a psychiatrist at the insistence of her primary care physician. The results of our clinical interventions were the interruption of her visits to emergency services, her willingness to go to work without expecting to die, and her increasing feeling of mastery over her life. Though she has occasional symptoms, she is able to deal with them without new medical interventions. Now, Edna is a well-accomplished fifty-five year old grandmother and a bank teller. Given the results of numerous research studies with anxious and depressed patients, we expect that there will always be a number of patients who have both anxiety and depression concurrently.

Josephine had had two episodes of postpartum depressions; she told us that the second time around, she was much better prepared, could recognize the symptoms, and could seek treatment early enough. We know that postpartum depressions happen more often among patients who have a family history of depression, have been depressed before, are depressed at the time of delivery, and experience stressful situations during pregnancy. Many patients, like Josephine, who have had postpartum depressions also suffer from other episodes of depression independently of pregnancy and delivery.

There are patients who are never free of depression, even though they have not had a full-blown episode of the disorder. Mabruka, for instance, experienced a chronic feeling of sadness, intermittently accompanied by other manifestations of depression, which did not amount to a full syndrome. She had a dysthymic disorder that, as is often the case, eventually became a major depressive episode, which led her to seek our attention. As so many other patients with both disorders, effective treatment for her major depression led to freedom from manifestations of anxiety, and a much better life.

Kent presented a difficult diagnostic challenge because his disorder started with bizarre ideas rather than with typical manifestations of depression. A patient with this type of disorder is likely to show in time the typical clinical manifestations of depression; even though the patient himself may deny that there is anything wrong. Unfortunately, the patient's thinking may lead him far away from reality, and his perception of himself and others may be completely erroneous. We were sad to see that Kent never accepted that he was ill, that his assessment of his ideas was wrong, and that his distorted ideas left him open to the worst outcome of a depressive disorder.

SUICIDE

When a patient dies by his or her own hand, something also dies in those who have been taking care of that person. Most mental health professionals have clear memories of every patient who took his/her life, no matter how long it has been since the suicide occurred. Considering that 15 percent of patients who have suffered from depression eventually take their lives, suicide will continue to be a major theme in any book that deals with depression. This is more so when careful studies of people who completed suicides show that the overwhelming majority of them were depressed at the time of their death, had often announced their intention to kill themselves, and had made the kinds of arrangements typical of those who are about to die.

We do not know when Kent decided to kill himself. We think he saw his parents' visit as the opportunity to get out of the hospital and commit suicide. His actions in the days preceding his death suggest that he had acquired a purpose, was laying out careful plans, and was going to deceive all those involved in his care. In retrospect, he had two of the characteristics of patients who are determined to commit suicide: hopelessness and telescopic vision about the future. Hopelessness seems to be the main link between depression and suicide. Hopelessness leads to lack of vision about alternatives to death. Telescopic vision focuses the patient on his own death. Writers have often described the situation in very telling ways: "Once a man decides to take his own life he enters a shut-off, impregnable but wholly convincing world where every detail fits and each incident reinforces his decision. An argument with a stranger in a bar, an expected letter which doesn't arrive, the wrong voice on the telephone, the wrong knock at the door, even a change in the weather—all seem charged with a special meaning; they all contribute" (See Note 3–1). When a serious attempt fails, the very suicidal event seems to take the patient out of the suicidal frame of mind. Armando, for instance, was an example.

Armando had decided, at the age of 34 years old, to kill himself far away from all the people he knew. He went into the countryside, parked his car several miles away from the nearest town, walked into the bushes, put his gun into his mouth, and pulled the trigger. The bullet destroyed much of his tongue, the palate, most of his nose, and his left eye, before coming out of the frontal bone without touching the brain. Armando heard the noise produced by the gun, felt startled, then felt covered by blood, and rushed to his car as fast as he could, driving himself to the police station at the nearby town, from where he was transported to a major trauma center by ambulance. We saw him after several surgeries and at a time when he was expecting many more. By then he could breathe easily, talk with difficulty, and swallow slowly. He was a very good patient who, in spite of his severe mutilations, kept on counting his blessings for having survived. In the years that followed, he never was suicidal again.

After two suicide attempts, the writer, poet and social satirist Dorothy Parker wrote:

Rivers are damp;
Acids stain you;
And drugs cause cramp.
Guns aren't lawful;
Nooses give;
Gas smells awful;
You might as well live.

Suicide attempts and completed suicides seem to have a different distribution among our patients. Most people who attempt suicide are younger women. Most people who kill themselves are older men. Most people who attempt suicide use less lethal means. Completed suicides occur in people who jump from high places, or hang or shoot themselves. Suicide attempts occur in many psychiatric disorders. Careful studies of completed suicides show that most victims had depression, while a certain number had alcoholism. Recent traumatic events are more common among those in the minority who had alcoholism. Suicide notes in general are surprisingly uninformative; quite often referring to mundane and peripheral matters. On the contrary, there is a substantial literature by people who have fought through the years against their desire to die.

Suicide has been reported more often in some countries, but these countries are also the ones that usually keep better statistics. Our evaluation of clusters of suicides in the same family tends to show that suicide is underreported, and often common in families with a very high prevalence of affective disorders. We know of several families in which suicide has been a major cause of death through generations.

The same cultural factors that interfere with the diagnosis and treatment of most psychiatric disorders also interfere with the early identification and proper treatment of individuals prone to suicide. We have seen this very clearly when we have examined the circumstances surrounding the death of individuals who were never diagnosed with depression, clearly had depression, and had an untimely and mysterious deaths.

Some people disappear after leaving clear written indication that they are contemplating suicide. That's the case of the writer and adventurer Ambrose Bierce, immortalized in the movies by Gregory Peck in *Old Gringo*, and who disappeared in Mexico in 1913 supposedly going to fight Pancho Villa. Bierce had written an essay entitled "Taking Oneself Off."

DEPRESSION IN CHILDREN

Our roster of patients for the day showed that the next patient was John Doer III. The person who came into our office was a very friendly and clearly pregnant young lady. She informed us that she was delivering John Doer III in a few months, and wanted to start therapy in the hope that it was going to protect her son from depression. She indicated that she had suffered from severe depression. She was adamant about her need for therapy for herself as well as for her son's future. We were interested in helping her help herself and her son. Thus, John Doer III, represented by his mother, became our youngest patient ever. As of now, John Doer III is a very successful high school graduate on his way to a well-regarded university. He is an example of a patient with a family history of depression in several generations who may never suffer a depression.

Depression is a problem faced by many children. Suicide could be high among them, primarily among adolescents. Minority adolescents exposed to a culture that encourages independence and that favors individual pursuits away from the parents, may move away from their own culture to try to be similar to other adolescents. In the process, they may hang between the culture of their parents, which they consider too old fashioned, and the culture of other adolescents which they do not find appealing or helpful. Joining a gang is often a very unfortunate solution. Among migrant Latinos, several studies have shown that the generation at risk for emotional problems is the second one in the new country. The migrants adjust, survive and thrive, but their children may not follow through and may, thus, fall by the wayside.

Rogelio

Rogelio was a timid, self-effacing, quiet, and worried student. He was referred to one of our mental health clinics because he had gained excessive weight and was the victim of every bully in the school. To begin with, Rogelio didn't want to be Latino. He didn't want to belong elsewhere, and certainly not with his tormentors. Rogelio was sleeping and eating too much; he had no energy, no interest in school, and no ability to concentrate. In addition, he had a number of other clinical manifestations that we clearly associate with childhood depression:

- Low grades in most subjects
- Rejection of school
- Isolation from other students
- Hostility towards his family
- Frequent accidents and injuries
- History of bedwetting
- Numerous pains, including headaches

Rogelio responded well to therapy, especially when antidepressant medication was accompanied by weight loss.

DECLINE AND DEPRESSION

Giovanni is one of our favorite patients. In 1950 he moved with his young wife to San Diego and opened his barbershop. Fifty years later he became forgetful and started to complain about the dryness of his eyes. He also began to sleep too much, and, contrary to his lifelong habits, he started to neglect his appearance. His primary-care physician told his family this was not unusual in a seventy-six year-old man who had been working all his life. However, one of his six daughters insisted that he come to our mental health clinic. Her main reason was that in the past we had successfully treated her for depression.

For some time, we have operated a day care center for patients with Alzheimer's disease. We learned much more at this center than we had ever expected: We learned that a decline with Alzheimer's disease is not necessarily uniform. Many patients retain some of their abilities. And one of the frequently observed, early clinical problems is depression.

We argued in favor of keeping the barbershop open. Giovanni was likely to retain his manual skills for many years; there had been at that point no complaints about his skills. His customers loved him, and his prices were by far the lowest in town. We also argued in favor of trying to maintain all of his routines, including his participation in ball games at the local park. We nevertheless advised Giovanni that he should not drive and, thus, should relinquish his driver's license. He seemed relieved when he did so. We had a number of interactions with Giovanni's primary-care physician, who was not convinced that Giovanni should take medications for Alzheimer's disease or antidepressant medication. When Giovanni started to take the SSRI fluoxetine, he and several of his children blamed the manifestation of eye dryness on this medication, even though it had been present before he began to take fluoxetine. We conducted a literature search to prove that dryness of the eyes had not as yet been associated with the use of antidepressant medications.

In the first few months of treatment, we received frequent calls from Giovanni's numerous children about supposed new symptoms that, according to the primary-care physician's previous clinical notes, were not new. After much discussion, we finally agreed that only one child would speak for the family. This greatly facilitated communications.

Many of our patients with Alzheimer's disease were born speaking a language other than English. Some forget English even though they have spoken it for many years—fifty years in the case of Giovanni. During our first interview, it was clear that Giovanni's wife spoke English quite well, but Giovanni answered most questions in Italian. This was not a problem for the children because Italian had been spoken at home all along. We decided that everyone in Giovanni's house was going to speak only English to him. As is the case of other persons who suffer from depression, the depression improved, and the memory partially returned; Giovanni began again to communicate in English.

Giovanni has now been our patient for four years. He still works at his barbershop and plays ball in the local park. He wears a bracelet with his name, address, and telephone number. We have color-coded a number of relevant objects and appliances at his home. We have also implemented a daily period during which he discusses recent events and daily occurrences with the family. Giovanni no longer complains about depression, takes his medications daily, and seems to enjoy his life very much.

Elderly minority patients will continue to increase their presence in every medical practice. They are subject to the same losses, ailments, and financial difficulties as other elderly persons do in this country. Depression and suicide are serious risks and require vigorous and effective interventions. The results are often surprising as in the case of María Estela.

María Estela

María Estela was seventy-six years of age when we first treated her for depression. Small amounts of fluoxetine were not effective; so we gradually increased the daily dose until she responded well at 60 mg daily. Through the years, we made several attempts at reducing the medication, but the symptoms of depression would return. When not depressed, María Estela, an accomplished singer, had been able to make several videos and tapes for her family, in which she narrated many treasured events. She has also recorded her rendition of many Mexican songs. Nowadays, at the age of 103, she still takes fluoxetine, and comes to our office every three months.

The decrease of morbidity and the gradual extension of longevity have created a new group of older people who are healthy and want to remain so. Some are already talking about becoming centenarians and super centenarians. They deserve all the clinical research needed to assure the continuous quality of their lives. As we understand them better, we have to think of new initiatives to guarantee the same care and opportunities, especially for the elderly ethnic minorities.

A FINAL WORD ON DEPRESSION

We want to summarize some of our thoughts about depression and ethnic minorities.

Depression tends to be under-diagnosed and under-treated among ethnic minorities. This is not only the result of lack of financial support for health care. Prejudice, discrimination, and ignorance are also big contributors. Any effective action to remedy this situation has to include a major increase in community awareness.

When treated, patients with depression tend to go to professionals who may focus only on the somatic symptoms and, thus, are unable to make the diagnosis of depression. The patients themselves may be more satisfied when the somatic symptoms of depression lead to an inappropriate diagnosis of a medical illness. The treatment, based on an incorrect diagnosis, is likely to be wasteful, and also contribute to the belief that medical treatments are not useful. Additionally, many ethnic minority patients do not believe that their treatment can be successful. When the depression is accompanied by hopelessness and helplessness, the patient may enter treatment with very low expectations, which may subsequently contribute to lack of compliance and early termination of treatment.

Depression is advancing to second place on the list of illnesses leading to disability. Depression that is neither identified nor properly treated is more likely to produce poor performance at work, absenteeism, and unemployment. These are precisely the factors that stop minority workers from successfully competing in the work market. The realization of the influence of depression on job performance is likely to help in obtaining early identification and effective treatment.

We need to continue to talk to community leaders, public policymakers, and influential ethnic minority advocates about depression. The five key points to remember have remained the same for several years:

1. depression is very commonly observed,
2. depression is easy to recognize if one thinks of the diagnosis,
3. depression can be or is often accompanied by severe disability,
4. depression can be lethal, and
5. depression can be successfully treated.

CHAPTER FOUR

TWISTING REALITY
Schizophrenia and Other Psychosis

Ruth

Ruth was a very elegant, sophisticated, intelligent, and ambitious woman whom we met, seemingly by chance, a number of years ago. We were doing field studies for diagnostic criteria for depression, bipolar disorder, and schizophrenia. Not far from our offices, down the same wing in a large university-affiliated hospital, two researchers about to become well recognized for their work on human sexuality were recruiting persons interested in learning more about their own sexuality. Ruth came to learn more about her sexuality, took the wrong turn in a hall of the hospital, and ended up in our offices. Her introduction to our secretary suggested that she was interested in research to know herself better, which was precisely what we were doing. She didn't mind that our systematic interview was thirty-six pages long and required one full morning to be completed. (Note 4–1).

Ruth was born in Panama, in a family that was predominantly Black, with the usual Latino mixture of many bloods; thus, her dark skin was accompanied by blue eyes and red hair. Having grown up in Panama City, she was fully fluent in Spanish and English. The family of an engineer at the Panama Canal, who was returning to St. Louis, Missouri, invited her to visit the United States. Ruth completed high school and went on to college and law school in the United States. In the process, she married another law student, and, a few years later, in her late twenties, they had two children.

In her late teens, and in order to help support herself, Ruth became a waitress; and subsequently, worked in several restaurants, cocktail lounges, and nightclubs. In her early twenties, Ruth started what she described as her double life. Every two years she had periods, usually lasting weeks or months, of increased energy, enhanced sexual drive, more interest in other people, and greater desire to dance the rhythms of the Caribbean, which had been part of her childhood and adolescence. During these periods, she would become Rosita, an exotic tropical dancer who soon became popular in adult clubs. She would marvel at her ability to study hard, get good grades, and still spend the night in her new activities. The periods of high activity would usually end suddenly; and, in the following weeks, Ruth would feel unhappy, threatened by the consequences of Rosita's activities and ready to promise to herself never to give in to Rosita again. Now, in our office, she wanted to consult about her sexual drive, which she thought was the explanation of Rosita's behavior. Her anxiety about this problem was increasing because the episodes seemed to occurring more frequently.

When we showed Ruth our diagnostic criteria for mania, she immediately identified the criteria as the characteristics of Rosita. Our impression was that Ruth suffered from a bipolar disorder. She had had several episodes of mania. During such episodes, she would act according to her enhanced activity and mood, her enhanced sense of well-being, her impulsivity, her grandiosity, her lack of inhibitions, and her decreased need for sleep or for rest. We thought that her symptoms created a reality for her that was not in accordance with her life when she was not manic.

Ruth accepted our clinical impression as well as our suggestion that she be treated with lithium. She had no new episodes of mania during the following three years. She proposed that we reduce and then discontinue the treatment. Three months later, while taking 300 mg of lithium daily, Ruth came to the office as Rosita. She said she wanted us to see her the way she was when manic. She looked like a different person. Her appearance suggested she was ready to enter a beauty contest. Her hair and her makeup made her look several years younger. Her clothes were far from the conservative business suits she usually wore. She was flirtatious, talkative, and uninhibited. She was also willing to increase the lithium again, and soon she went back to her usual life.

Dr. Assad

Dr. Tufic Assad seemed to be always active and always involved in many projects. In a city that enjoyed a substantial number of eye surgeons, he wanted to be the busiest, the one who worked in all the hospitals, and the one who had the largest number of operations in one day. His enthusiasm was contagious, and his colleagues usually accepted and followed his ideas.

A clinical psychiatrist would have recognized that Dr. Assad had pressure of speech, flight of ideas and remarkable grandiosity. These manifestations were quite clear the day he presented his plans for the new eye institute, his brainchild, with numerous operating rooms, video cameras, a spa, a restaurant, auditorium, and a tele-medicine center. The enormous building seemed a geodesic dome, and represented a complete eye globe. Those of us practicing in the vicinity and practically everyone on the staff of the big adjacent hospital were invited to become members of the eye institute. The proposal called for the members to pay dues every year, so that we could keep up with the most recent inventions at the eye institute. This proposal had to be shelved because of lack of interest.

The inauguration of the eye institute, which coincided with the beginning of excavations for the building, was a social success, attended by a substantial crowd. The inauguration seemed to also mark the beginning of the end of the project. Even while the round walls were emerging, there were cost overruns, changes in architects and contractors, dissension among the future occupants and co-owners of the building, and numerous legal actions leading to bankruptcy and the closing of the project. Later, we met Dr. Assad at a psychiatric unit of a local hospital. He was severely depressed.

THE FACES OF MANIA

Both Ruth and Dr. Assad suffered episodes of mania that led to excessive behaviors not necessarily identified by most persons as manifestations of illness. Ruth and Dr. Assad enjoyed their episodes of mania, but not their aftermath. Ruth had realized that her behavior during an episode of mania, was destructive, while Dr. Assad thought that he was at the peak of his professional and business career, although he was displaying behavior produced by mania. Ruth described at least mild depressions at the end of her episodes of mania. Dr. Assad had a major depression that required hospitalization.

Seven manifestations are typical of mania. At least three are necessary for the diagnosis:

1. Inflated self-esteem or grandiosity
2. Decreased need for sleep
3. Being more talkative than usual or under more pressure to keep talking
4. Flight of ideas or subjective feeling that thoughts are racing
5. Distractibility
6. Increase in goal-oriented activity or psychomotor agitation
7. Excessive involvement in pleasurable activities that have a high potential for painful consequences

Each of these manifestations is common enough in the general population to make the diagnosis difficult, and more so among people whose history is not readily available. The diagnosis may be close to impossible in patients who use or abuse stimulants as well as other drugs that alter the person's emotional states. Psychosis is often identified by delusions, hallucinations, or bizarre behavior. Mania may or may not be accompanied by psychosis. Other disorders that we are studying in this chapter include manifestations of psychosis.

Adhana

Adhana was very tall, had a regal bearing, and often wore colorful clothes that looked like those worn by many people in central Africa. He always sat alone, and seldom talked unless answering a question. Early in our interactions, all the answers to our questions were very concrete and preferably about the weather. He seemed to hate any reference to himself or to any other people. At least one of our psychiatric residents, thinking that Adhana had come from Africa, suggested that his limited vocabulary and his concrete answers were because he was still learning English. It so happened that English, or at least the English spoken in the small communities of southern Louisiana, was the only language Adhana had ever spoken.

We met Adhana at the park where we usually pick up patients for our homeless program. When we asked him whether he wanted to come and work with us, we interpreted his silence as a positive answer. When he brought his meager belongings to our first interview, we also interpreted his actions as indicating that he wouldn't mind if we were to find a shelter or other accommodations for him. Doing what we considered appropriate every time he did not talk, we seemed to advance slowly at first and more rapidly later.

Adhana started to speak more after we gave him antipsychotic medication. As we increased the dosage, Adhana started to talk more about himself. Eventually he seemed to remember parts of his life. He had grown up in a town of fishermen. He didn't think he had gone to school. He did not believe he had been married. He didn't know how he came to the west coast. He had no memory of many years of his life. He thought that he could have been in the Navy. The diligent work of one of our social workers permitted us, by trial and error, to find a last name that Adhana recognized as his own. Our social worker checked with the Veterans Administration (VA), on the assumption that Adhana had been in the U.S. Navy or had been admitted to a VA hospital. This initiative led us to a medical history and to a military record.

Adhana had gone to high school near New Orleans. He had joined the army and had made it to staff sergeant before he was admitted to a military hospital because of a psychotic breakdown. During the breakdown, he kept on seeing animals threatening him and kept on claiming that his brain had been destroyed. After several months, Adhana received a medical discharge with a service-connected disability and was referred for outpatient treatment with antipsychotic medications.

The medical records showed that Adhana had several admissions to psychiatric facilities in twelve different VA hospitals. The location of these hospitals suggested that Adhana had been traveling often. The most recent admissions had been separated by periods of many months. Adhana had been described as unable to remember his past history and had often been transferred to the VA hospitals from jails. He had often been accused of vagrancy, loitering, and threatening other people. He had not been known to be violent.

Living in board-and-care homes, taking substantial amounts of antipsychotic medications, and attending our partial hospitalization program, Adhana became much more talkative and slowly started to tell us more about himself. He had never worked after leaving the army, had never been married, had moved from town to town with no clear purpose, and for several years, not had a clear idea about his identity. It also turned out that Adhana's VA pension and his social security benefits had gone uncollected for years. With the help of several agencies, we were able to obtain an assigned payee, who received a substantial amount of money for Adhana.

In time, Adhana was able to move to his own apartment, bought a full wardrobe, bought all kinds of appliances, and seemed to start living a relatively prosperous life. However, he was still socially iso-

lated, trusted very few people, and was very aloof in all of our therapeutic activities. His verbal production was also very concrete, and
his affect was always flat. When Adhana started to insist that the time
had come for him to go back to Louisiana, we suggested that he visit
several times, for at least one week each time, before he made the
final move. We helped him to get living quarters in southern
Louisiana and arranged with the nearest VA clinic to provide follow-
up care for him. He promised to send us a postcard when he arrived
at his new home. He didn't do so. The landlord reported that Adhana
never showed up. The VA lost track of him once more.

Andres

After the state hospitals and other psychiatric facilities that gave asy-
lum to the mentally ill in our town were all closed, all sorts of board-
and-care homes emerged near our general hospital. The most colorful one was City Manor, a place that had been a hotel, and eventually
became a dilapidated building, full of patients with severe and persistent mental illness. City Manor was a place never to be forgotten
by many of us. It was a trading center for drug users, a hangout for
prostitute handlers and their clients, a bartering center for clothes,
stolen goods and other paraphernalia, a place where anyone could
crash at his/her own risk, and the abode of forty or so people who
usually suffered delusions and hallucinations. Their medications
were often colorfully displayed in the nearby trash bins, their clothes
changed owners enough to be called community property, and the
place was self-contained only because the police patrolled it often
enough to forestall a massive exodus.

We often visited City Manor, or at least the few sections of the
building that didn't seem to be about to collapse. There we met
Andres, then a cantankerous, semi-naked, hyperactive, youthful individual who spoke his own mixture of English, Spanish, and his own
neologisms. Andres didn't know at the time that thirty years later we
would still be trying to communicate with him. One day, City Manor

collapsed out of decrepitude, mismanagement, pestilence, and the weight and influence of the many agencies that were investigating it. As is often the case with facilities for people with mentally illness, the closing of City Manor didn't cause any ripples in the community. Some of the tenants became denizens of the city's largest park; some retreated to spaces under the bridges, highway bypasses and nearby buildings and some simply died. Andres was rescued by one of our social workers, who cleaned him, gave him acceptable and appropriate clothes, and found temporary quarters for him at a shelter for homeless people.

We were eventually able to talk to the owner of a small, well-managed, board-and-care home whom we convinced to accept Andres as one of the six occupants of three small bedrooms. We also brought Andres to our partial hospitalization program, and started efforts that are still ongoing to help him to accept the reality shared by other people, to talk only in one language at a time, to improve and enhance his daily living activities, and to move at least in part from his own convoluted reality.

Andres finally accepted a shot of haloperidol decanoate in one of his arms every month for more than twenty years. He attended many team meetings concerning his care with counselors, dietitians, rehabilitation counselors, and specialists in internal medicine. He has also been amused at our family interventions. After Andres left City Manor, we found his mother's address. We visited her. She said that Andres was her favorite son out of twelve. She was sorry that she had lost track of him when he was twelve and left home.

Patricio was the brother who seemed to care for Andres. He explained to us that the brothers were for freedom, for opportunity, and for a balance in living their own lives. He himself was a butcher and saw a balance in killing cows so that others would eat. He promised to always retrieve Andres, no matter where he went. Andres had traveled and visited many places since we got him into his board-and-care home. After violating all of our rules, Andres roamed through Mexico, at least through most of the states of the

Mexican Union, and faithful Patricio had always retrieved Andres, usually a bit dirtier, thinner, and more confused than at the beginning of his expeditions.

We believe there are many communities of patients with schizophrenia who are quite different from their usual portrayal in movies. We find many patients with schizophrenia loyal to a few principles of friendship, generosity, and often helpful to each other. We would not have been able to serve as many patients as we have were it not for patients who often guided each other to our offices, shared their minimal financial resources, and found ways of enhancing each others' lives.

SCHIZOAFFECTIVE DISORDER

Many describe Francisco as stilted, eccentric, unusual, idiosyncratic, or "a character." His mother suffers from periodic episodes of depression and has come to our office intermittently for many years. We first met Francisco via a photograph because his mother wanted us to see him receiving multiple awards while in high school for his high scholastic achievements. He eventually obtained a degree in mathematics from one of the most prestigious universities in the country. Subsequently, he spent six months in a psychiatric hospital experiencing delusions and hallucinations. After he improved, he became a clerk at a county primary-care clinic. After a few years, he was again admitted to a psychiatric hospital, this time, depressed and delusional. After his discharge, he went to live with his mother and received vocational rehabilitation, learning to repair computers, which he did for several years. After a third depression with psychosis, he was not able to work for several years. He now distributes newspapers many mornings. He loves this activity, is very good at it, and takes pride in it. He has never been married, has no friends, and leads an isolated life, in which his mother is the center of activity. We seldom see Francisco, and he only accepts medications when severely depressed. He has never had an episode of mania.

Kathy, to the contrary, is a bubbling volcano who is always taking generous amounts of antipsychotics, mood stabilizers, and, from time to time, antidepressants. She is an accomplished painter, but has not been able to support herself for many years. She has many transient friends but does not have any steady relationships. Hospital records show that she has not had any clear change in her demeanor or her symptoms in many years. She gets admitted to psychiatric hospitals when she becomes too expansive, delusional, and/or belligerent. She usually leaves the hospitals when her family is willing to cope with her. Making a case for social security disability for her was not difficult.

We reserve the term schizoaffective disorder for patients who experience repeated episodes of depression or mania concurrent with psychotic symptoms superimposed on a course of illness that suggest a schizophrenic disorder.

PSYCHOSIS AND ALZHEIMER'S DISEASE

Tony

We already spoke about Giovanni, our long-term patient with depression and progressive decline in his intellectual functions. We also discussed María Estela, who developed depression in old age without intellectual decline. We now have to address a different clinical problem.

In a neighborhood where there are almost as many people from the Philippines as there are Latinos, Tony seemed to belong to both communities. He often mentioned his Spanish name as clear evidence that he was even more Latino than his neighbors: "My great-great-grandfather came from the Philippines before anybody knew about America." Tony had been a guerrilla fighter and later an army officer in World War II. He could not miss any military parade because he had to display his medals: "The best way of educating the youngsters is telling them what we did for them."

It was not Tony but his wife who first came to see us. She explained that, for some time, Tony had been forgetting the places where he had left his belongings, especially his beloved uniforms and his medals. He had gone from losing them, to accusing others of stealing them, to taking protective action, to converting his home into a virtual fortress. Despite our old friendship, Tony wouldn't come to our office: "[You] may be in on this."

When we came to visit Tony, he was a changed man. He took us into a closet to confide that he couldn't talk in his bedroom because he believed the enemy had planted microphones in it to spy on him. He explained that a group allied with the old Japanese imperial government had arrived in our town intending to kill every veteran, and, because he was a prime target, he was taking measures to protect himself and his family. Though fully delusional and losing his memory, Tony accepted our medications: "After all, this is what friends are for. I'll help you so that you can help me."

THE MANY FACES OF PSYCHOSIS

Adhana, Andres, and Francisco had a chronic, progressive psychiatric disorder accompanied by delusions and hallucinations. The disorder affected their behavior, their interactions with others, and their ability to support themselves. When we talk about this disorder constellation of psychotic and other types of symptoms, we are referring to schizophrenia. This is not the only psychiatric disorder that produces a psychosis. We have already referred in Chapter 3 to the psychosis that Karen suffered as a result of bipolar disorder. In cases like hers, it is easy to see that the clinical manifestations of mania and those of psychosis tend to co-occur.

During the course of their disorder, patients with schizophrenia may also have episodes of depression, usually of a much shorter duration than that of psychosis. Depression among young patients with schizophrenia is often accompanied by suicidal thoughts and behaviors. Only recently, have we come to acknowledge, based on research efforts, that schizophrenia is a major risk factor for suicide.

Patients with long-term psychosis and shorter periods of mania or depression are usually diagnosed as having schizoaffective disorder, as in the cases of Francisco and Kathy. Disorders of the brain, particularly those produced by drug intoxications, metabolic disorders, vascular problems, tumors and degenerative disorders, are often accompanied by psychosis. In our experience, the largest and most challenging groups of patients are those intoxicated with drugs or suffering from Alzheimer's disease.

The most difficult patient in the memory of many staff from our mental health clinic was an anesthesiologist. He was referred to the psychiatric intensive care unit of a nearby hospital after showing up at the hospital while hyperactive, grandiose, and clearly experiencing vivid visual hallucinations. His blood toxicology screen tested positive for alcohol, amphetamines, and barbiturates. He vigorously opposed admission, had to be restrained, and was placed on twenty-four-hour observation. On the third day of his hospital stay, he talked to his psychiatrist about how embarrassing it was for him to take care of his daily needs in front of the staff while they watched him. He requested to be transferred to a private room where he would be observed every five minutes. With smiles and strong words of assurance, he explained that he was not going to kill himself and could easily sign a contract acknowledging that. After his transfer to a private room, he was observed for about three hours reading in bed when the nurse came into the room. Then, he succeeded in hanging himself from the doorknob, in a room where there was no other way of doing so. For this purpose he used the bed sheets, which he had been tearing apart while supposedly reading.

PSYCHOSIS AND THE ETHNIC MINORITIES

Working in neighborhoods where ethnic minority individuals live, we have not observed any difference in the incidence, prevalence or clinical characteristics of schizophrenia. As expected since the sociology studies of the first part of the 20th century, patients with schizophrenia tend to drift towards the poorer areas of our cities. While participating in studies of the genetics of schizophrenia among Latinos, we have been able to trace the same disorder in several generations of the same family; quite often, we had to locate patients' relatives in several countries. It was typical for these people not to know that they were related to a patient with schizophrenia.

As happens with patients with depression, pessimism and fatalism often interfere with the diagnosis and treatment of our Latino patients with schizophrenia. We have had the opportunity to diagnose several cases of schizophrenia in families that were maintaining secrecy about the existence of the disorder and leading chaotic lives in the midst of distress and turmoil. It was usually members of the extended family, neighbors or community groups that brought the problem to our attention. The interventions that led to treatment success usually proceeded slowly, with much cooperation from outside decision makers.

The best opportunities for effective treatment tend to occur when relatively intact families have been prepared to support the treatment of our patients. Andres' mother was full of promises about helping us with him, but she didn't even come to the phone when we tried to get them talking. In contrast, brother Patricio didn't mind traveling long distances by plane in order to retrieve Andres after some of his visits to faraway places. We often marveled that Patricio had more difficulty going through customs, airports, and many cities than Andres ever did.

We can't stress enough that the behavioral factors that contribute to early physical diseases, chronic physical disability, and early death in the general population are also present among patients with schizophrenia, including those belonging to the ethnic minorities. Many of these schizophrenic patients tend to be overweight, many smoke cigarettes in large amounts, many do not exercise, and many follow diets that tend to produce unhealthy metabolic conditions.

Regarding the lack of exercise, the same lack of volition and initiative that hinders social adaptation contributes to extremely sedentary lives. Unhealthy diets occur even in the presence of healthier foods.

Clarence, a remarkable African-American patient, was a stout forty-six year-old gentleman with a twenty-year history of admissions to VA hospitals, where he had been treated with phenothiazines, apparently with no change in blood sugar levels. Within a few days of taking 400mg/day of chlorpromazine at our hospital, his blood sugar went to 185 mg /100 ml. When we cut chlorpromazine to 200 mg/day, the blood sugar went down. This experience led us to study a random sample of 850 patients (Note 4–2) treated in the same hospital with phenothiazines. From this group of 850, 823 kept normal values of blood sugar. Among the remaining twenty-seven patients who showed increases in blood sugar, five developed permanent hyperglycemia.

This early study, which we published in the *American Journal of Psychiatry* almost forty years ago, has kept our attention focused on the problems of sedentary, overweight patients who take antipsychotic medications. The full story probably includes numerous factors, but there are a few measures that we would like to focus upon. They are as follows:

1. Become aware of your patients' height, weight, blood sugar, and blood cholesterol at the beginning of treatment.
2. Become aware of your patients' dietary habits and make every effort to influence them. We favor some interventions because we can definitely show they have been effective in the treatment of other patients with psychiatric problems. We must acknowledge, however, that information about dietary strategies has to be frequently repeated to the patient, and also given in writing.
3. Try to encourage exercise. This is a very frustrating endeavor. In a recent experiment with extremely obese, chronic psychiatric patients, we distributed free pedometers to ten patients who were willing to commit to increase their

daily walking. Half never used their pedometer. The other half included only one patient who used the pedometer for about two weeks and subsequently discontinued its use.

As we try to modify habits and behavior among our patients, we may remember that poor attention span, poor concentration, and resistance to change tend to be common among most of our patients.

LESS COMMON PSYCHOSIS

The diagnosis of schizophrenia specifies that the person experiences the symptoms for at least six months. A patient who has a psychosis that resembles schizophrenia and enters treatment within the first six months of the illness will receive the diagnosis of schizophreniform disorder. A patient with symptoms suggestive of schizophrenia for a period as brief as one day to one month who later improves will be diagnosed as suffering from a brief psychotic disorder.

A FINAL WORD ON SCHIZOPHRENIA

The prognosis of schizophrenia is not uniformly poor; many patients may have only one episode, while other patients, like Francisco, may have repeated episodes with relatively slow social deterioration. A minority of patients may have a severe, chronic disorder with multiple symptoms that last for many years, like Adhana and Andres.

We have periodically surveyed our practice with respect to the distribution of psychiatric diagnoses. Patients with schizophrenia are fewer than 5 percent of the new referrals to our practice. Nonetheless, if we do a cross-sectional study of the patients attending our practice, they are usually 20–25 percent of the patients regularly coming to our office. This clearly results from their being much more chronic than other patients and having needs that keep them close to us. As opposed to patients who have suffered from depression and other psychiatric disorders, patients with schizophrenia often need help with housing, transportation, diet, daily activities, care for comorbid physical conditions, relationships with their families, and occasional legal matters. They also have problems that deter less committed colleagues from accepting them as patients. For this and other reasons, there is a lack of mental health professionals willing to treat people with schizophrenia.

Regardless of optimistic calculations by some agencies, we are convinced that there is a shortage of psychiatrists in the United States. This shortage is becoming more critical and affects the ethnic minority populations more often than other ethnic groups because of many barriers to care, including lack of medical coverage.

We want to stress that all ethnic minority psychiatrists should pay special attention to patients with schizophrenia, even if this requires seeing them for minimal fees, frequently spending long periods of time in hospitals, long-term care facilities, and board-and-care homes, as well as acting as primary-care physicians for patients with severe psychoses, several chronic physical illnesses, and multiple social problems. Abandoning the care of patients with schizophrenia means, to a large degree, the abandoning of those who need the most during a time when state and federal policies have made them almost completely invisible.

We continue to applaud the policies of the American Psychiatric Association (APA) that give priority to community care and to community efforts while attempting to provide adequate care for the most serious psychiatric disorders.

CHAPTER FIVE

TWILIGHT ZONE

Bud

Powerful Mr. Lightfoot was, he said, 100 percent Native American. He boasted that his family had been in Wisconsin long before it was a state and much before the first European had set foot in his ancestral lands on the shores of Lake Michigan. When we met, he gave us the impression that he knew everything and everybody. He was a short man with dark eyes and dark hair. By current standards, he could have been thinner. He was always very carefully and formally dressed. His appearance was part of his current role.

Bud Lightfoot had been born on the reservation. He had been raised by his paternal grandparents because his father had died young from cirrhosis of the liver, and his mother had left to go to Chicago and seek a different life. The grandfather had been an excellent source of support, and the grandmother had been very nurturing until her death during Bud's early adolescence.

With good recommendations and grades, Bud had gone to high school in Milwaukee. He told us his years there were a blur of drinking, fighting, being suspended and expelled, and being given new chances. After a series of arrests for disorderly conduct, driving without a license, and driving while intoxicated, a judge gave him a choice: a long period behind bars or military service. Bud didn't last long in the Army. He soon began drinking again, went into increasingly long episodes of drinking, and finally went AWOL. He was discharged after three months. Once a civilian again, Bud went into intermittent construction work, constant smoking, heavier drinking, numerous arrests for driving while intoxicated, and finally a return to Milwaukee, where he took residence, or rather, lack of residence, on skid row.

One day Bud woke up in jail and was told he was being accused of murder. Someone had been stabbed to death in the proximity of the street where Bud was sleeping. Without memories, alibis, witnesses, or even someone who could testify for him, Bud was sentenced to eleven years in prison.

Bud narrated the ensuing events in his life as follows: "This enormous old Indian, twice my size, mean looking and with a thunder for a voice, came into my cell two days after I arrived. He introduced himself as the prison chaplain. When I introduced myself, he said, 'Mr. Lightfoot? Baloney! I am Mr. Lightfoot. I am a decent, hardworking man from the prairie. You are a lousy bum from Milwaukee, who happens to share my name.' Probably he was correct in all of that. He also said he was a recovering alcoholic and would try to talk sense into my mind and soul . . . if at all possible." The two Lightfoots started this way a relationship that lasted until the older one died. Bud, the younger, received through the years, an education in Alcohol Anonymous (AA), a sponsor, an opportunity to attend regular meetings, and much more: a sense of dignity, a need to learn, a lifelong sobriety, and eventually, a degree in social work.

We met Bud when we started our practice and told a number of colleagues we wanted to treat alcoholics. Bud became a permanent companion. We would go together to the emergency departments, the jail, and the recovery homes. He invited us to open AA meetings, and there we founded new alliances with people who had been in much more difficult circumstances and often had many years of sobriety. Through the years, Bud became a guide, advisor and close friend. He showed us the internal workings of AA, from a successful intervention, to support during detoxification, to the twelve steps, to the twelve step calls, the meetings, the camaraderie, and the sorrows.

Johnny

Johnny came in the office by himself, indicating that he was in the neighborhood, was interested in talking with a psychiatrist, and wanted to know whether we thought it was time to leave his home. After all, he was thirty-eight years of age. When we asked whether anyone else had a say on the decision, he mentioned his mother was also interested in talking to us. The mother, Mary, happened to be in the waiting room.

It turned out that Johnny had spent a total of fifteen years in a number of jails and prisons. Together with two years in mental hospitals, Johnny had been away from home a lot.

Johnny had started using amphetamines when he was twelve years old. By the time he reached fifteen, he had accumulated a history of driving without a license, driving while intoxicated, leaving the scene of an accident he had caused, truancy from school, assaultive behavior at school, and being expelled from all the schools he could attend. High on amphetamines, he went to a grocery store, picked up two cans of beer, left the store, and was about to open the first can when he was arrested for a number of infractions. This is why he spent three years in juvenile facilities. During this time, free of drugs, he graduated from high school.

As an adult, Johnny left Juvenile Hall with drugs in mind. His first purchase was videoed and introduced in evidence for a new arrest. And so Johnny's life kept on going. From drug deal, to arrest, to jail, to prison, and to increasingly limited periods in the community.

Johnny's mother was a physicist at a research company. She had been born and raised in China, the daughter of American missionaries. At the university she had married a fellow physics student. The marriage worked well until she decided to come to work in the United States. Johnny's parents separated and grew increasingly distant, until they finally opted for a divorce. Mary's nuclear family was Johnny, to whom she gave enormous amounts of love.

Mary looked much younger than her fifty-eight years. She was a no-nonsense physicist who didn't mince any words: The system had mistreated her son. What had initially been attributed to adjustment difficulties after coming to the United States at an early age, turned out to be a learning disability that Johnny still suffered. His drug use and antisocial acting-out seemed unplanned and unexpected acts did not make sense for years, until Johnny developed delusions and hallucinations while in prison and away from drugs. Mary had enough financial resources to have Johnny evaluated at excellent psychiatric centers, where she was told Johnny's main disorder was schizophrenia. Mary didn't know of any history of psychiatric disorders in her own family. At the insistence of Johnny's psychiatrist a few years back, she had asked her ex-husband about instances of psychiatric care in his family. Johnny's father was, like Mary, very matter-of-fact. Yes, there were people in the family whose behavior couldn't be explained. Some of them had ended up unable to support themselves, often living in poverty. No, there were no psychiatric hospitals in the distant chinese provinces where they had lived.

Mary told us Johnny had been released from prison six weeks before. He was taking an antipsychotic that dissolved in his mouth, so that she was sure he was getting the therapeutic effect.

Our interview with mother and son helped clarify several issues: According to the mother, the parole conditions included that Johnny live with Mary and take the antipsychotic medication. Mary displayed her daily graphs, no doubt a product of her research training, showing that Johnny's intake of street drugs rapidly declined while he was taking medications. Mary had already established connections with the National Alliance for the Mentally Ill and with several programs interested in the rehabilitation of psychiatric patients.

Aurelio

Our friend at the coroner's office called. Our name was on the medication bottles for Aurelio. The coroner just wanted to check on a few facts. We wanted to come to the place where they had found Aurelio, which turned out to be his nice apartment downtown.

Aurelio's last trip was really the last. He died with a syringe still sticking out of the last vein he had found on his hand. The needle was still in the vein, showing Aurelio's expertise, corroborated by all the tracks on most of his body.

Aurelio had been a restless high school student. With little effort, he made good grades. He was into sports, many social activities, low-riding cars, and enjoying his life to the hilt. His classmates introduced him to marijuana. He found it weak and dangerous, because it would put him to sleep while driving.

But heroin was something else. He described his first experience to us: "I was really scared. I didn't appreciate piercing my body with someone else's needle. The beginning was as I expected . . . I had a rush of fear, and feared a total loss of control. My heart pounded, I couldn't breathe, I was going to explode . . . and then, it was nirvana. . . . I no longer needed to open my eyes to see beautiful plants, birds, skies, and, above all, peace, ecstasy . . . the ultimate experience of happiness. I would do anything to come back here."

Aurelio did anything and almost everything to go back there. He discovered that a steady but increasing supply of heroin would permit him to act normally while feeling the effect of the drug. As his needs increased, the same amounts of heroin would not give him the exalted feeling he had expected, but would permit him to stay ahead of the new problem: withdrawal. The fear of withdrawal gradually replaced the need for any pleasure. He found that not long after missing a "fix," his whole body would revolt: he would experience palpitations, chest pain, nausea, vomiting, abdominal cramps, diarrhea, weakness in all his muscles, and extreme exhaustion without being able to sleep. The fear of the symptoms motivated his search for the drug.

Aurelio gradually moved from consumer, to dealer, to distributor. His life became embedded in heroin. He was arrested a number of times for possession with intent to sell. By now he couldn't afford the lawyers who kept him out of prison. He several times went to detoxification and rehabilitation centers. He became familiar with clonidine, naltrexone, and other compounds we used in detoxification and long-term treatment of addictions. Though he had them, he seldom used them with any consistency. He never developed a commitment to staying away from heroin. To the contrary, he would go to extreme lengths to obtain the heroin that he thought was the least diluted. This probably killed him: the heroin that usually came to town had been mixed several times with other substances that increased the volume and decreased the concentration. The day of his death, someone had given Aurelio almost pure heroin. A dose that he thought was the usual killed him. He was thirty-one years of age.

Juan

His name was Latino, but he argued this name had been with the tribe from before the time the Spaniards came to his place. We had no chance to argue with Juan that the name of the tribe, clearly a Spanish name, and his own name were part of the domination by the Spaniards for the best part of several centuries. Our problem was that Juan smoked three packs of cigarettes a day, had emphysema, and soon would not be able to breathe at all. His position was that he should be allowed to be himself, as if destroying his lungs was being himself.

The time came when we visited Juan at the hospital when he had an oxygen tank by his side. He invited us to talk at his retreat. Much to our horror, his "retreat" was a balcony in the ward for those dying from inability to breathe. The balcony was the last resource for those dying in the hospital from cigarette smoking who wanted a last chance to destroy their lungs. They could go to the balcony for a few cigarette puffs, knowing it was a short distance from their oxygen tanks.

Juan was a living—or dying—demonstration of the strongly addictive capacity of nicotine and perhaps some of the many poisons added to tobacco in order to create the modern cigarette.

Hosni

Hosni's parents were a totally integrated couple. Both were linguists, who often shared their academic work and writing. They were charming socialites who often entertained at their home and enjoyed sharing it with their friends. The rumor was that Hosni's mother, Madeha, had been a distant cousin of King Farouk of Egypt. She and her husband had been married in their native land, had completed their degrees in Europe, and had come to the United States with their only son.

Hosni had done very well at an excellent high school, until the senior year when his grades plummeted and he seemed to start living in a world of his own. One day Hosni exploded and claimed that his body was possessed by the body snatchers and he was no longer himself. After admission to a psychiatric hospital, tests revealed that he had been ingesting lysergic acid diethylamide (LSD). He admitted that he had been consuming hallucinogenic drugs for several months. Treatment in the hospital was successful in controlling Hosni's psychosis, but he came back home listless, uninterested in school, and seemingly unable to find himself. Soon thereafter he was using the same drugs and developing the same symptoms. After another hospital stay, he went to a thirty-day recovery program. He came back home promising to attend at least one group meeting each day for ninety days. Within one week he had dropped out of the program and was using drugs again. He went back to the hospital for detoxification, and this time he accepted referral to a long-term residential facility where a rehabilitation program was available.

ADDICTIONS AND THE BRAIN

We believe the mounting evidence that addictions have a brain representation, and that imaging, using positron emission tomography (PET) and other techniques, will permit a better definition of brain events that perpetuate addictive behavior. This is made starkly obvious when just the presence of a needle with heroin produces in the heroin addict the same transmitter discharges as the actual use of cocaine. Similarly, the alcoholic has the same discharges when approaching his favorite tavern as he would if actually drinking alcohol.

Evidence collected in recent years leads us to believe that repeated administration of addictive drugs produces marked and long-lasting alterations in the functional activity of the mesocortico-limbic dopamine system, particularly in glutamate and dopamine transmission in the nucleus accumbens. (Note 5–1). This evidence has led to treatment strategies based on better knowledge of brain reactions to drugs.

We can easily support the use of drugs such as naltrexone, whose action stops the transmitter discharges associated with addictive behavior. We expect that more complete understanding of the neurology of addictions will permit more targeted and more successful treatments than we have today. We'll come back to this theme later in this chapter.

As we mentioned in Chapter 1, genetic and cultural factors frequently go together in influencing psychiatric disorders. We believe this is true for addictions.

THE MANY FACTORS THAT MAY INFLUENCE ALCOHOLISM

Chris told us he grew up hating alcohol. Both his parents drank daily and often to oblivion. They mistreated each other and their children, were often intoxicated and often without recollections of the insults and the fights. Chris protected himself by spending much time with friends and with nondrinking relatives in a large African-American community. Chris didn't drink at all until he became a high school senior at the age of seventeen.

One night, Chris went to a party with his classmates. As usual, he was drinking a soda, when his peers started teasing him for not drinking beer. "For this once," Chris decided to have one. Since then he never stopped. Narrating the event later, he said, "Not long after the first sips, I was a different man. All my anxiety was gone, I was much more certain of myself, I could join the group, I could make jokes, and I thought I had finally become myself. I thought I had been missing a lot for not drinking." Chris had a history typical of someone with many heavy drinkers in the family; he went on to follow the life history of the American alcoholic: starting as a teenager, drinking more in his twenties, having serious social problems in the thirties, receiving care for medical problems related to alcohol in the late thirties, and being identified by himself and by others as an alcoholic between ages forty and fifty.

Sons of alcoholics are more likely to become alcoholics if they are reared by their drinking relatives than if they were separated from those relatives shortly after birth and are reared by nonrelatives. Adoption studies are corroborated by studies in twins. Identical twins are significantly more likely to be concordant for alcoholism than fraternal twins.

In a given individual, separating nature and nurture is not easy. Chris may have had a lesser chance of becoming an alcoholic in a culture that frowns on alcohol use. After all, two conditions to initiate an addiction are that alcohol be available and be used. Then, the metabolism of alcohol is modified by factors that can be inherited. Alcohol doesn't need to be digested and is readily absorbed in the gastrointestinal tract. Though extrahepatic tissues also participate, ethanol is oxidized mostly in the liver, to acetaldehyde by alcohol dehydrogenase. Acetaldehyde is further oxidized by aldehyde dehydrogenase.

The genes most likely associated with alcoholism encode alcohol dehydrogenase and aldehyde dehydrogenase. Two alcohol dehydrogenase genes (*ADH2* and *ADH3* on chromosome 4, and one aldehyde dehydrogenase gene (*ALDH2* on chromosome 12) exhibit functional polymorphisms that influences the rate of alcohol oxidation.

The *ALDH2*2* polymorphism, prevalent in Asian populations but not common elsewhere, has the strongest protective value against alcohol dependence. Those homozygous for this polymorphism have close to zero risk for alcoholism. In one study of Native Americans, those with alcohol dependence were significantly less likely to have the *ADH2*3* allele and significantly more likely to have the *ADH2*1* allele. The *ADH3*1* polymorphism, prevalent in Asians, Caucasians, and African Americans, may be associated with a lower risk for alcohol dependence. Many believe that polymorphism at different loci may not occur independently. Those isoenzymes that produce a faster metabolism of alcohol and a more rapid production of acetaldehyde should increase alcohol sensitivity and a reduction in consumption. (Note 5–2).

Our increasing understanding of factors that influence the metabolism of alcohol may one day explain that even though as many as 70 percent of adults in the U.S. consume alcohol, most never become addicted to alcohol. One day we may base our interventions in support of children at risk with the help of genetic markers for increased risk of alcoholism and other addictions.

NALTREXONE, CLONIDINE, AND BUPRENORPHINE

In this section we are not going to talk about these compounds as therapeutic agents in chemical dependence. We want to emphasize that research advances are moving our thinking towards combining psychosocial measures with agents that change events in the central nervous system so that we have a better chance of success.

Bud and Chris were likely born with a genetic susceptibility to alcohol addiction, and rapidly became addicted. Bud became abstinent with the help of a powerful counselor and an almost total immersion in AA for a number of years, the faith in AA as the only hope for those with alcohol addiction was practically unchallenged. Other psychosocial strategies have emerged that also offer promise. At this point, we want to refer to developments involving addictions and the brain.

The most recent history of efforts at using narcotic antagonists to effectively block the euphorigenic and dependence-producing properties of opiates can be traced to the 1960s. By 1973 the National Institute on Drug Addiction was supporting numerous grants to study narcotic antagonists. Most of them were on the use of naltrexone. By 1977 it was becoming clear that naltrexone would be of help to at least a small proportion of individuals addicted to opiates.

Several pivotal studies in the early 1990s led the Food and Drug Administration (FDA) to approve naltrexone, an opioid-receptor antagonist, for the treatment of ethanol dependence. The initial suggestion was that naltrexone substantially increased sobriety and reduced alcohol consumption when combined with psychosocial treatment. The premise was that stimulation of the opioid receptor contributed to the rewarding effect of alcohol.

Clinical trials with naltrexone in the treatment of alcoholism have been inconsistent. Until we have more information, the recommendation is that physicians continue to prescribe naltrexone for patients that might benefit. These seem to be those who have been drinking for twenty years or less and have stable social support and living situations. (Note 5–3). Those favoring the use of naltrexone remind us that alcoholism is a chronic illness in which relapses are to be expected. Naltrexone-treated patients have been known to drink less and take longer to relapse. (Note 5–4).

Clonidine, a centrally acting alpha-adrenergic agonist, came to be used to treat opioid withdrawal because of a known series of events: opioid drugs are agonists at the opioid receptor, where they inhibit cyclic AMP systems. When chronic opioid use is discontinued, the cyclic AMP system in noradrenergic neurons becomes overactive and brain activity increases, contributing to withdrawal symptoms. These neurons also have adrenergic auto receptors that, when stimulated by clonidine, decrease neuronal activity and reduce opi-oid-withdrawal symptoms. The use of clonidine has permitted many psychiatrists to treat patients withdrawing from heroin in settings where this was not possible before. (Note 5–5).

Though we were quite impressed with the original research on the treatment of heroine addicts with methadone, we were clear that the initial reports referred to the successful treatment of carefully selected patients, including those with higher education, better social and educational adjustment, and higher motivation. At least in the places where we have lived in the last decades, methadone clinics failed to live up to their expectations and often were used to exchange opiates among people with minimal motivation for absti-nence. We were therefore quite encouraged when, in the last ten years, buprenorphine, an opiate agonist-antagonit, emerged as a new option for treatment of opioid dependence.* (Note 5–6). The obsta-cles imposed by the regulators seem to have kept most psychiatrists from using buprenorphine, so that the jury is still out about the future place of this compound in the practice of those who treat minority patients.

THE DRUG WARS

Though the treatment of individuals who are suffering addictions continues to be neglected, and current preventive action is generally ineffective, many billions of dollars have been spent in destroying marihuana plantations, coca fields and poppy plants, and many more in interdicting the traffickers, sending the distributors to prisons for long periods, and trying to eliminate drugs from the streets of America. There seems to be a consensus that this war has been far

---

* Though buprenorphine has been approved for clinical use, the psychiatrists interested in using it need to be certified and are required to follow specific rules, which suggests that widespread use is not likely as of the time of writing of this book.

from successful every year for many years. The casualties have been many. Any visitor to the prisons that hold drug offenders, practically all of them young, will realize that the minorities are excessively represented among the war casualties.

Drug dependence is the unique situation in medicine where psychiatric problems combine with questionable strategies to send minorities into the penal, rather the mental health, system.

Carlos likely suffered an episode of bipolar disorder when he was fifteen years of age, which was when he became disruptive in school, impulsive, and belligerent. He was soon using marijuana, amphetamines, and cocaine. Like most of the people we have known who use stimulants, he would take alcohol or benzodiazepines to "come down." A combination of frequent intoxications with several drugs, disregard for rules, and avid pursuit of dangerous challenges led to numerous encounters with the police, repeated incarcerations, and several long stays at the local penitentiary. In the process, he learned to smuggle street drugs into prison, use IV drugs with other inmates, and participate in the immense drug trade existing behind bars. Carlos became infected with the hepatitis B virus, developed several other infections, and almost died before his last release, when he was thirty-two years old.

Martha, Carlos's mother, reacted with shock, disbelief, and then anger, as she saw him become sick, weak, isolated, and oblivious. Martha thought that many years of Carlos' life had been lost because he was in the wrong system. She expressed her ideas as follows: "From the beginning, it was like a fight between two forces: a powerful business versus a feeble and poorly organized nonsystem. The Department of Corrections, a powerful multibillion-dollar enterprise, wanted my son when it became clear that he had become a nuisance. He was never identified as sick or as a human being in need of protection. He was an enemy of society that had to be removed into the horrifying entrails of a monster that would dehumanize and destroy him. The alternative would be to use the mental health system. What system? Here, in our society, we forget that mental illness and secondary drug dependence do exist. If we have a choice, we charge the person and put him away from society, no matter that doing so is much more expensive and has no visible beneficial effects. Today, in our town, the largest mental health hospital is inside the state prison."

Martha and other mothers joined with many advocates to try to change the situation in California. They proposed the state referendum Proposition 36 that would give courts the opportunity to offer treatment when having to sentence nonviolent individuals with drug dependence. The voters approved Proposition 36, which is now being implemented. It is an instance of effort by many people to separate users from the traffickers and others that are destroying them.

Most mental health professionals agree that treatment offers a brighter future than the police efforts to remove drugs from the streets. As long as there are eager consumers, there will be sellers and distributors. Even more, maintaining a habit of heroin, cocaine, or amphetamines is beyond the financial means of many addicts, so that the alternatives are to obtain funds by illicit means, or to start selling and distributing, as was the case with Aurelio. Either alternative is tremendously costly to our communities.

Aurelio once told us, "I opted for selling, recruiting potential sellers, and starting to distribute. Soon I had earnings that went beyond my dreams. At the beginning, I had a relatively steady bill of $150 a day. To have that much, I had to steal $1,000 a day, which meant breaking into cars and houses, stealing anything I could remove, and pawning, selling, or destroying it the same day. Going up in the distribution chain was so much easier."

We need to provide early, effective, and affordable treatment to all people with drug addiction. This treatment has to be accessible and community-wide. It has to be integrated with programs for other psychiatric and medical disorders and should be designed so that confidentiality is respected. Short of this, we may be contributing to the belief that treatment can't be effective.

There are many reasons why minorities have a primary interest in treatment reform. Our youngsters are languishing in prisons when they should be part of our future. All in the community suffer when an important percentage of those who use drugs may resort to damaging everyone to support their habit. The losses to the community are increased by the belief that problems in the larger community are necessarily related to problems in the areas where the poor live, and the belief that belonging to a minority group is the same as being sentenced to poverty and squalor.

CHAPTER SIX

TALKING PSYCHOTHERAPY

Vickie

During our first interview, Vickie said she had always known she was attractive to men, but that was part of the problem. She had not always made the right decisions about them, and now felt as if she had to undo most of the decisions she had made during a period of several years. By all appearances, Vickie was an example of a person who had succeeded in life. After working at the central library for several years, she went to work at one of the new biotechnology centers that were populating the valley close to the local university. That's the place where miracles seemed to happen, where drugs with spectacular effects originated, where new technologies and approaches to medicine were emerging, almost on a daily basis. The match seemed to be perfect. Vickie displayed the same qualities that made her shine at the library, including her care for each person's concerns, her painstaking interest in the most minimal details, and her desire for precise documentation of every significant occurrence. She soon became the personnel manager at the laboratory complex.

Joseph (Joe) was in charge of one of the key laboratories. Not long after Vickie arrived, he was solicitously showing her around,

helping her meet new people, and discussing with her the best strategies for the company. In less than six months they were dating, and a
few months later, he proposed marriage, and she accepted.

Vickie and Joe were soon happily married, or so it seemed. He
happened to have the same ideas about his home as he had had for
years about his well-run laboratory. He expected Vickie to respect all
his decisions about everything in the house, to pay all her expenses
out of her own checking account, and to contribute exactly half of the
monthly budget. When they decided to buy a house, he unsuccess-
fully tried to place it in his own name "as head of the household." He
also, without Vickie's input, planned all the vacation time, often
around attendance at sports events that were dear to him. Vickie
gradually lost all her former friends, because now her social life was
with Joe's old group, which went back for many years. Vickie's older
brother, an artist living away from home and quite sick, came for a
week to pay Vickie a last visit. He cut it to three days when Joe made
it clear that he was not welcome in their home.

Though increasingly disappointed, Vickie wanted to get pregnant, in part because she felt the situation would change if a baby
were around. After a wait of three years, they underwent fertility
testing and eventually chose in-vitro fertilization. Vickie went alone
through the process because Joe was too busy. She finally became
pregnant. However, when she had a miscarriage, Vickie had to go to
the hospital alone. This seems to have been the last straw.

She soon started thinking of a divorce. Life got complicated for
Vickie after she mentioned her unhappiness to her husband. She felt
as if she had been suddenly fired. Joe immediately stopped effective
communication about most subjects, although he did start talking
about how he had found and bargained for their house, therefore it
was really his; what Vickie had paid, half of the monthly installments,
should be considered as rent. He also proposed to give back her half
of the down payment.

One day, when communications were at a minimum, Vickie
packed her clothes and left to stay with Alina, one of the few friends

she still had. Now, she feared Joe was going to accuse her of deser-
tion. Alina found a lawyer for her, and Vickie filed divorce papers.
Life at the lab became increasingly difficult, but Vickie decided not
to quit until she found a new job. Her credentials as a manager and
administrator were superb; thus, she soon had a number of alternative job offers. There was a university branch nearby that needed a
personnel manager immediately, which meant that she could be
hired practically on the spot. But then, suddenly, she collapsed; she
was completely exhausted, unable to think or to concentrate, unable
to make plans, and unable to make decisions. That's when, through
the good services of Alina, Vickie set an appointment to come to our
mental health clinic. Vickie was tearful and evidently upset when she
came to the office. She was, nevertheless, very nicely dressed, very
articulate, presented her problems clearly and precisely, and was
willing to use any help we could provide at that time. Vickie's immediate problems were acute, but the history indicated that they also
were a continuation of other ongoing difficulties.

Her parents were born and raised in Argentina and had moved
to the United States shortly after being married while in their early
twenties. Vickie's maternal family had come to Argentina from
Ireland two generations before. They shared a strong commitment to
the Catholic Church, as did the family of Vickie's father, which came
to Argentina from Germany.

Vickie's parents came to the United States accompanied by a
number of siblings and cousins; thus, the family became a growing
group of closely related individuals. Two of Vickie's Uncles eventually
achieved successful academic careers as university professors, while
her father became a lifelong union representative and leader. He was
an electrician. Her mother devoted her life to her family. She was
high-strung, suffered anxiety about minimal situations in life, and
appeared to be chronically depressed. She died before Vickie's
father. Two of Vickie's older brothers were quite different from one
another. One was an easygoing artist who died in his thirties, and
Vickie idolized him. She still has many of his pictures in her house.

The other brother was a high achiever who became a colonel in the Army. He later had a second career in the civil service. Vickie also had two older sisters. Both married young and had children. One of them, a boy, was later diagnosed as suffering from schizophrenia, a disease that ran in the family of the boy's father. Vickie's younger brother, always very close to her, and a very successful electrician, also became a very successful general contractor.

Vickie remembers her mother as always aloof, always worried, and always unable to express her feelings. Any support Vickie had during her childhood came from her father and her younger brother. Though today one might say Vickie is the star of the family, when she was growing up, she tended to perceive her sisters as being more beautiful, intelligent, athletic, and popular. She also perceived herself as the ugly duckling, even though it was clear that she was the one who attracted more boys and was really popular in many places. She now remembers not hearing many positive comments from anybody in the family, except occasionally from her busy father and her very quiet younger brother.

Vickie thinks of her teens as being very unhappy years. She felt she didn't belong to any group, was often sad, and didn't expect much from the future. She was seventeen years old when one of her cousins died in an accident. This tragic event led to a big commotion in the family. Everyone dressed completely in black for several days, and time seemed to stand still for several weeks. Her cousin's funeral was the most important ceremony Vickie had ever attended in her life. Yet, at the time, she remembered, she couldn't stop thinking that she would rather be the cousin, cold, lifeless, and beautifully smiling in the coffin.

During and after high school Vickie worked in as many jobs as she could find, starting in fast-food outlets, going on to waiting tables at restaurants, helping a friend who ran an apartment complex, and looking for a more stable position. In the process, she learned that she had a very good mind for computers, accounting, administration, and planning. Once she made it to the library, she excelled in her tasks, which opened the doors for the research company.

All along, her social life was determined by family affairs or invitations by co-workers. She seemed to run into men who didn't have much to offer or men who wanted short and inconsequential relationships. Even though she dated several of her male friends for many months, the dates were infrequent, and Vickie would take steps to avoid closer, intimate relationships. In this regard, she was similar to some of her friends, who wanted to learn more about life before they became finally committed to someone. Vickie's relationship with Joe changed her perspective; she had wanted to be a housewife and a mother. Beginning with a full commitment to her marriage, Vickie went from hope, to disappointment, to pessimism, and finally to a deep need for a new orientation in her life.

GOALS IN PSYCHOTHERAPY

Vickie responded well and rapidly to antidepressant medications. In a short time, she was no longer having crying spells, was sleeping better, had better concentration, was not as anxious, and became ready to commit to a reorganization of her life. We appreciate the efforts of the psychotherapists who believe that all psychotherapy is geared towards achieving a better future. The basis for this thinking has been cogently expressed by psychotherapist Bernard D. Beitman and his colleagues: "Individuals compose expectations of the future from prior experiences within their culture, developmental norms, and the early events of their own life. The brain registers the sum of one's experience and uses this material to rehearse future ways of thinking-feeling-doing-living; this procedural memory becomes the foundation for mental movies of one's future, or *Expectation Videos*." (Note 6–1).

In preparing to offer a better future to Vickie, we could distinguish several themes in Vickie's life that warranted revisiting:

1. Lifelong tendency towards depression and pessimism
2. Poor self-image
3. Lack of self-confidence
4. Unclear personal goals
5. Pain of a failed marriage, preceded by a miscarriage
6. Expectedly bitter divorce
7. Beginning of a new and better life

There were many reasons for us to believe that cognitive strategies offered excellent long-term psychotherapy possibilities for Vickie. She was a clearly intelligent person who had spent time writing and analyzing ideas from other people. This was the basis for her success in personnel management. She was an insightful thinker who usually developed new ideas to address old problems at work. She also had succeeded in addressing and resolving problems for others in areas that she had usually left unfilled in her own life. (Note 6–2).

In Vickie's family, there were numerous examples of highly successful people, including university professors, her father as a respected union leader, her brother who had obtained a high position in the military and in civil service, and her brother who had become a successful contractor. Their feats were the talk of the family. Vickie, however, saw herself as a hard-working and reliable person, who was plodding along without much distinction. She had a clear all-or-nothing approach to life, which seemed to keep her on the "nothing" side. Since childhood, she had become used to not expecting much, so she tended to disqualify her achievements, passing them through a filter that stressed her negative aspects. She never thought about the fact that she was doing well in the same positions that were occupied in the past by people with higher education. She often felt that she didn't deserve as much as they did. Her line of thinking kept her focused on whatever went wrong; thus, she had no doubts that she was the major contributor to the failure of her marriage, even though there were many facts that could lead to the opposite conclusion.

For Vickie, it was a surprise to discover that she might have been depressed for most of her life, and that this may have contributed to her pessimism, poor self-image, and lack of self-confidence. While in psychotherapy, it was easy to point out that all these themes could be tied together. If she were to have a more positive view of herself as an attractive, intelligent, sociable, and very reliable person, she would have to try for more, see herself as more deserving, and trust herself in deciding about her future career.

For the short-term, at the beginning of our interactions, we focused on her reactions to the worsening conflict with Joe, the dissolution of her marriage, and the impending transition to a new job. (Note 6–3). We saw our goals as helping her see the advantages of the job transition and accepting her new challenges. This gave us an opportunity to explore her current feelings about Joe. Better insight led her to an appreciation of his shortcomings and the limitations he had imposed on her. This generated a growing rejection of the past that represented a desire for a more fulfilling life. She had been happy with her job, but understood that working with Joe at the same company while going through a divorce might not be the best situation for her. It turned out that she was less dependent on her job than she had originally feared.

The university branch that hired Vickie was rapidly growing in the areas of organization, department structure, and personnel. Vickie arrived at a time when planning was moving fast into implementation; many academicians and administrative staff were being hired, and she was at the center of much activity and rapid change. On the job, she found herself making decisions constantly and trying to think today about the realities of tomorrow. This was very helpful in decreasing the tensions produced by Joe's constant demands about the divorce settlement, in which Vickie was barely able to retain some of the heirlooms she had brought into the house. Eventually, she was glad to sign the divorce papers.

OUTCOMES

Several years have gone by, and Vickie has positively changed a great deal. She now recognizes her value and her potential. She knows she can make and keep new friends; she knows that she is appreciated and admired. She has come to the conclusion that her perceptions of people during her childhood may have been tinted by her depression. She is now a leader in her work setting and an active participant in the lives of her many friends and many nieces and nephews. A favorite young niece relishes playing the role of Vickie at Vickie's home and at the office. Vickie's life and personal goals have changed. She has become much more independent, buying the house she wanted and making plans to invest in other properties that she will manage herself. She expects to receive promotions as the university expands. She no longer feels that she has to rely on others to define her own future. She also believes that having been depressed can be used to create new commitments based on the opposite: the desire to enjoy life.

PSYCHOTHERAPY AND MINORITIES: THE MYTHS

Those who have wanted to engage ethnic minority patients in ongoing psychotherapy have faced a number of difficulties in trying to dispel the myths many minorities have about themselves and about psychotherapy. These self-defeating assumptions are examples of emotional thinking and of jumping to conclusions without evidence, which hinder the progress of ethnic minorities because the assumptions drain the energy that should be used to work on future perspectives.

1. **I am what I am.** This is a common problem. Vickie told us about June, an ethnic minority staff member at her university office. Vickie was upset that June behaved as if she had been hired to be June; that is, a person with a minimal school achievement, a limited occupational background, and a limited interest in others, but fully committed to defend the rights of ethnic minorities. As an ethnic minority person coming from one of the poorest neighborhoods in

the city, June seemed to expect that the unsophisticated, the coarse, and the empty should have a position on the university staff because these people represented the poor. Vickie was unhappy that June acted as if the negatives should be used to present the case for ethnic minorities. Vickie felt, as a self-made person and as the daughter of immigrants who came to the United States with very little, and as a person who now takes pride in herself, that she should challenge June and demand the best from her. In the end, June accepted counseling.

2. **It is for a reason (God gave this to me)**. There is a frame of mind that goes against verbal therapies and that can be presented in many ways: a) If I feel the way I do, I probably deserve it; b) Pain comes from sin. If I have pain, I must have sinned; c) There is an order to all that happens to us. I probably have what I deserve; and d) I do not understand all that is happening. It may be the will of God.

3. **There are forces I'll never master**. Among ethnic minorities, especially among those who have migrated recently, the world may be seen as controlled by powerful forces that act beyond the reach of the individual. Whether it is the migration authorities, the local or state government, the federal rules, or even the regulations controlling traffic, the minority person may see society as ruled by immutable and perhaps sacred mandates that are often incomprehensible. Here, we see examples of magnification, making potentially bad situations bigger than they are, and emotional reasoning, attributing negative feelings to events that may not be true. This is quite clear in situations when migrants do not even send their children to school because of fear that the family will be harassed on account of immigration rules. Situations like this need to be frequently addressed during psychotherapy.

4. **It's they and we**. This is one of the most corrosive myths, in that overgeneralization and labeling are used to justify negative events and situations by indicating that the individual doesn't belong to the group in power; thus, he has nothing to expect from society. Individuals need to accept that inequalities, discrimination and prejudice exist, they are not the only forces moving a community, and they are often balanced by countervailing positive forces.

5. **Psychiatric care is for crazy people**. At least among Latinos, a common believe is that the only people who ever go to see a psychiatrist are those who have lost their minds. The farther away the person is from psychiatrists and psychiatric facilities, the more he or she may entertain unrealistic beliefs. We have already talked about using community leaders, advocacy groups, and all those interested in health to advance the mental health of the community. A favorable outcome should be that ethnic minority groups avail themselves of psychiatric care, including psychotherapy, in the same proportion as other population groups do.

6. **Psychotherapy is not effective**. All the evidence coming from carefully conducted studies supports the opposite view. That is, targeted psychotherapy has been proven to be effective in most psychiatric disorders. In the ensuing paragraphs we will talk more about psychotherapy among the patients we have introduced in earlier chapters.

BREAKING THROUGH THE BARRIERS

In Chapter 1, we left three of our patients in Miami. Let's revisit them:

Mr. Louis Petion had a major depression with psychosis that led him to believe he had been hexed. He came to the United States fully convinced that he had to protect himself. His symptoms, including loss of appetite, loss of weight, lack of sleep, loss of energy, and difficulty pursuing his usual activities, led him to a clinic, sponsored by Cuban immigrants where his condition was diagnosed. A counselor, whose French was compatible with Mr. Petion's dialect and who had experience with beliefs common in Haiti, explained the wonders of modern medicine in removing the effects of ill will. A combination of antidepressants and antipsychotics seemed to do the rest, and Mr. Petion was happy to report that he was recovering from his hex. The remaining problem was that he wanted to return to Haiti, at a time when the trip was impossible and not advisable.

Mr. Petion's requests to be sent back to Haiti were not different from Ms. Lopez's demands to be returned to her home in Mazatlan, Mexico. Ms. Lopez had been virtually dragged into a community family center, where an astute worker pointed out that the pain she experienced after her husband's death had lasted much too long, had incapacitated her, and had prevented her from paying attention to the living, including her solicitous children. As is often the case among Latinos, Ms. Lopez would not initially accept the idea of going to see a psychiatrist, but was willing to follow the recommendations of a primary-care physician, who, in turn followed the suggestions of a consulting psychiatrist. After the treatment started, the psychiatrist also saw Ms. Lopez at the primary-care clinic and eventually was able to refer her to our mental health clinic.

Mr. Petion and Ms. Lopez were both ideal candidates for our group activities. We have found that migrant patients, no matter where they come from, bond with each other, share many activities, and enjoy exploring their new country together. Because of their age, they share problems like loneliness, isolation from others, worries about physical health, and lack of confidence in the future.

Helped by her children, Ms. Lopez has integrated well with the large Mexican community in their neighborhood. Mr. Petion has done likewise with the Haitian community. They both are now less committed to their eventual return to their country of origin.

Ms. Brown is about to finish her training as a registered nurse and wants to become a psychiatric nurse. She attends our mental health clinic at irregular intervals, depending on her needs, which mostly relate to stresses at work and concerns about a possible recurrence of her depression, which has not happened.

ANXIETY DISORDERS

Both Mabruka and Abram in Chapter 2 suffered from manifestations of anxiety. Mabruka would suffer anxiety symptoms when she was depressed. Abram had had anxiety and also obsessions and compulsions before he was depressed. Neither situation is uncommon. We all know that anxious patients often want immediate help. We can use this urgent need to benefit the patient. Over the years, several strategies have emerged that have proven to be very helpful.

Pepe suffered a major depression with severe anxiety attacks. His devoted wife indicated that living with Pepe was impossible because she had to hold his hand all the time out of fear that he would lose control. We expected a good response to treatment because his three older sisters had suffered similar depressions that improved with psychotherapy and antidepressants. We chose to refer Pepe to our Anxiety Clinic while starting him on medications and longer-term psychotherapy. After a period of three weeks, Pepe was able to engage in didactic training sessions. (Note 6–4). Pepe first learned the relaxation response; he learned to regulate his breathing while working on progressive muscle relaxation. We used his progressive mastery upon his breathing to teach him to meditate while focusing on breathing.

We tend to agree with those who believe that the fear of fear is sometimes worse than the actual experience of an anxiety attack. This fear is often accompanied by fear of loss of control and fear that the next anxiety attack will have no cure. Teaching Pepe to monitor his levels of anxiety and examine the circumstances that made him more anxious helped him a great deal. His increasing mastery of breathing and relaxation to help control his symptoms, combined with the changing ideas about his anxiety, made a big difference in his attitude and self-confidence.

Abram

We gave Abram *Man's Search of Meaning*, the short book containing Dr. Viktor E. Frankl's contributions to psychiatry. (Note 6–5). Abram was very interested in the application of the Frankl concept "paradoxical intention." In the chapter on anticipatory anxiety, the book explains, "It is characteristic of this fear that it produces precisely that of which the patient is afraid." In paradoxical intention, the patient is invited to produce, even for a moment, precisely the symptom he fears. Abram was interested in practicing this technique. We first prepared a list of his obsessions and compulsions. We asked him to focus on each for about one week. He was to try to count as much as possible, check on each door not three but ten times, try to imagine the worst scenario in a number of situations, and try to focus precisely on the thoughts he found unacceptable. We were able to obtain results similar to those of Dr. Frankl and his colleagues in Europe: "Obsessions and compulsions decline and often disappear while the patient tries to focus his efforts in enhancing and repeating them."

PSYCHOSIS

We have described the emergence of psychoses in depression, in bipolar disorder, in drug addiction, in dementia, and in schizophrenia. Many cognitive and interpersonal strategies are successful when combined with somatic interventions in acute psychoses. There is growing evidence that chronic psychoses present challenges that often require complex psychosocial interventions.

Much has been written about the multiple cognitive, family, social, and vocational problems that hinder the progress of patients with schizophrenia. (Note 6–6).

Studies of family interventions are often based on concepts developed while studying patients with schizophrenia who return home. They often face "expressed emotions," such as criticism, over-involvement, and hostility. Though the jury is still out regarding the relative value of family interventions, our clinical impression is that the family plays a critical role in the treatment of ethnic minority patients with schizophrenia. This is more so when ethnic minority families tend to be more tolerant and to accept patients who still suffer severe symptoms.

Case managers continue to be major participants in the treatment of patients treated in ethnic minority clinics. Patients and their families are often unaware of the services that are critical to the community survival of most patients, and the case manager is the expert in linking patients with those who can help them.

We are often faced with ethnic minority patients who have gone through many years of neglect and relative isolation. Social skills training is often a requirement for other related services, including occupational training and vocational rehabilitation. Cognitive therapy has gradually made its way into the treatment of chronic patients with psychosis. Among patients with medication-resistant psychotic symptoms, new coping strategies and problem-solving interventions have led to targeted reductions in psychotic symptoms.

Adhana and Andres in Chapter 4 represented the multiple challenges that we encounter in treating long-term patients with schizophrenic disorders. Adhana got better, but then dropped out of treatment. Andres has remained in our programs, but we have had great trouble getting him to be better adjusted and more functional.

ADDICTIONS

Ethnic minority patients have successfully participated in twelve-step programs, intensive outpatient programs based on cognitive therapy, and reality-oriented programs that favor improvement in social skills and interpersonal relationships. When drug dependence is associated with another psychiatric disorder, adequate treatment for both disorders has led to a higher rate of success.

Do we often find lack of access to treatment for alcoholism and other drug dependence among ethnic minorities? The answer is a clear "yes." (Note 6–7). We'll discuss the problem further in Chapter 10. Here however, we can say that community awareness and training of ethnic minority experts on drug addiction are the first critical steps in changing the situation.

Can drug addiction be treated in patients who also suffer from other mental disorders? To many, it is a surprising finding that psychiatric patients with a history of drug dependence achieve abstinence. (Note 6–8). Critical to success is the identification and treatment of drug dependence in patients admitted for the treatment of a mental illness.

Can substance abuse be prevented in multicultural communities? Programs that address the large diversity of individual factors and environmental factors that influence drug addiction show that clinicians may learn to use a full gamut of interventions, usually targeted to each group and in accordance to their needs. (Note 6–9).

Finally, a warning: it has been shown (Note 6–10) that a large proportion of potential research subjects, including African Americans, low-income individuals, and individuals who had more severe alcohol, drug, and psychiatric problems were disproportionately excluded from alcohol treatment studies. In other words, before we apply any research studies to ethnic minorities, we have to find out whether they are relevant to the ethnic minority groups who reside in the United States.

PSYCHOTHERAPY FOR MINORITIES

For whatever reasons, some non-ethnic minority individuals think that psychotherapy is a European invention that has its best effect on people from European ancestry, whereas somatic therapies should be used for ethnic minorities. We find this opinion ill-informed and dangerous. Most evidence shows that interventions that appeal to emotions and to the will to change have a long tradition among all the peoples of the world. Our patients, no matter what their ethnic, racial, or geographical origin may be, respond well to all modalities of psychotherapy. We want to encourage those who share our opinion and our values in this regard to insist that all ethnic minority patients deserve the best treatment plans and that these plans often include psychotherapy in one or in many of its rich forms.

CHAPTER SEVEN

REMEDIES IN COLOR
Psychopharmacology

Olo

Olo, a thirty-nine-year-old engineer from Nigeria, came to the emergency room of a local hospital with anxiety and an inability to think clearly. He had lost his job recently because he could not perform well. He lived with his family but was worried about not being able to provide for them. His wife was working and supporting the family. Upon a psychiatric evaluation in the emergency room it was determined that Olo did not require admission. An outpatient appointment was made for him, and he received a prescription for 2 mg of risperidone daily. Olo had left Nigeria about fifteen years before, but kept in touch with his family at least once a month. He was also sending some money for the education of his younger brothers and sisters. Olo had two children, ages fourteen and twelve. They were both doing well academically and he was very proud of them. Education was important for the whole family as Olo had fulfilled his career dream because of his education. Olo's wife was supportive, but got frustrated as a result of Olo's lack of concentration, his hearing voices, and low motivation. Olo did not suffer from any serious physical illness and had no history of surgery. Family history was negative for mental or physical illness. Olo was raised in a middle-class family, and his needs were satisfied given the standards of his culture. He was a serious and good student, and was also considered to be a fun person.

Olo was assigned to a psychiatric resident who was working in the area of biology of ethnicity. He took a keen interest in helping Olo, so a good rapport developed between them. Risperidone was increased to 4 mg daily, without side effects. The resident then annoyed Olo by asking whether he was taking the medication regularly. The question made Olo feel that the psychiatric resident did not trust him. It was important for Olo to be trusted by the psychiatric resident, as Olo liked him. Olo remarked to the resident, "I have come here for help. I have a wife and children to support. I know I am ill. I trusted you to help me, but you did not trust me. Get the medication level checked in my blood." During the next visit, at 8:00 a.m., before he took the morning dose, Olo's blood sample was collected to estimate the risperidone and 9–hydroxy risperidone levels. They were both very low, and this explained why risperidone did not produce any improvement or side effects. Thus, three months after Olo started therapy, a conference was held to evaluate the results of therapy. It was agreed that Olo could be a rapid metabolizer, thus, clearing his medication very quickly and thereby not having an appropriate therapeutic level of the medication in his blood. After 20 mg of Paroxetine was added to Olo's regimen to block the CYP2D6 coenzyme, his blood level of risperidone on a dose of 8 mg daily was within therapeutic range. This led to a gradual improvement over the next two months and to Olo's discharge to return to work. (Note 7–1).

Lisa

Lisa, a very lean and weight-conscious thirty-year-old African-American female, was working as an X-ray technician. Lisa started hearing derogatory voices and responded to them by talking back.

Lisa did not provide a detailed family history. Accepting her reluctance, attempts were not made to find out more about her family. Lisa had not used alcohol or street drugs at any time. Physically, she remained lean and athletic; looking beautiful was essential to her. Lisa had difficulty concentrating, fulfilling her obligations at work, and was concerned that she might be making mistakes at work. At times, she was found to be gazing with a vacant look. Her mood was normal, but she showed some anxiety. Lisa felt that her work and self-sufficiency were important for her, and, thus, she wanted the voices to go away as soon as possible. The psychiatrist assigned to treat her prescribed 2 mg of risperidone once daily. Two weeks later, Lisa was found to be better subjectively. She mentioned that her voices had decreased by 70 percent. Her concentration and behavior had also improved. However, Lisa was found to be anxious and depressed with low motivation and lack of interest in her personal appearance. This led to the addition of 20 mg per day of fluoxetine and continuation of risperidone at 2 mg daily. Two days after fluoxetine was added, neighbors found her lying immobile and unable to swallow anything. She was brought to the local emergency room where she was noticed to be rigid and immobile, requiring an admission to the intensive care unit (ICU). Intravenous fluids and benztropine mesylate were administered in the ICU under the supervision of a neurologist; it took ten days in the ICU for her to improve enough to be transferred to the psychiatric ward. It is likely that Lisa was a poor or slow metabolizer and the addition of fluoxetine, an CYP2D6 inhibitor, slowed down the metabolism of risperidone and increased its blood level; thus, causing a severe extrapyramidal reaction.

Why are these patients different? The first patient, Olo, did not improve with the usual treatment but responded to the CYP2D6 inhibitor, paroxetine. Contrary to the first patient, the second patient, Lisa, developed a severe extrapyramidal reaction with 2 mg of risperidone and 20 mg of fluoxetine daily. The answer is that people from different ethnic groups have different genotypes for drug metabolism.

Olo was a rapid metabolizer, and Lisa was a poor metabolizer. These two cases show the need for understanding the alterations of metabolism due to genotype variations in different ethnic groups.

CULTURE AND ETHNICITY

We are going to refer here to individual and ethnic variations that affect drug metabolism (pharmacokinetics) or the way drugs affect different organs (pharmocodynamics).

Most studies report the core symptoms of schizophrenia to be similar across cultures. In a study of a large sample of indigenous Africans (Xhosas), the structure for the symptoms of schizophrenia were reported to be remarkably similar to that previously described among Caucasian patients. At the end, with the same symptoms, differences in outcome could be related to genetically determined pharmacokinetic and pharmacodynamic differences between different ethnic groups.

Ethnic minorities tend to live in low socioeconomic areas of their communities as a result of limited acquisitive power and also as a result of cultural differences. They have left behind their native support system and are faced with the support system of a new culture; that is, the majority culture. This creates an enormous tension. Ethnicity and culture may substantially influence clinical presentations, treatment responses, and overall outcomes of psychiatric disorders. While cross-cultural psychiatry was previously regarded as a little more than an intellectual curiosity, both ethnic and cultural aspects of psychiatry are now also recognized as important aspects of clinical psychiatry.

One reason for this is that clinicians in most countries increasingly have to manage ethnically diverse populations as the numbers of immigrants and refugees increase worldwide.

The revolutionary human genome project and recent advances in molecular genetic research have transformed the prospects of medicine by providing diagnostic tests for diseases, better prognosis of illness, and specific treatment options for individuals. Advances in this area of biotechnology have opened up the field of pharmacogenetics, which is defined as the study of variability in drug use and drug response due to genetic variability between individuals or populations. This domain has helped us to understand how drug metabolism, drug response, adverse effects, and clinical outcome can be related to the genotypes of individuals. In psychiatry, the importance of genotypes has been amply substantiated.

PHARMACOGENETICS: CYTOCHOME ENZYMES

Diversity in rates of response to medications can be explained by differences in the rate of drug metabolism, in particular by the cytochome P-450 superfamily of enzymes. (Note 7–2). Ten isoforms of cytochome P-450 are responsible for the oxidative metabolism of most drugs. Variability among patients in the activity of these enzymes is related to environmental factors and both genetic and nongenetic host factors. The effect of genetic polymorphism on catalytic activity is prominent for CYP2C9, CYP2C19, and CYP2D6, which collectively account for about 40 percent of drug metabolism mediated by cytochrome P-450. CYP2D6 has been most extensively studied. It is involved in the metabolism of about one hundred drugs, including antidepressant, antipsychotic, and opioid agents.

Distinctive differences are found across ethnic groups in the functioning of these enzymes, which lead to variability in the pharmacokinetics and drug response to psychotropic agents. This is due to biologic differences in individuals, as well as interethnic differences among them. Pharmacokinetics is considered as the most significant factor in inter-individual differences, which are in turn related to genotype variations, which can nowadays be measured.

The genetic variations in drug metabolizing enzymes result in different levels of metabolic functioning, which are classified into four different phenotype groups. The normal or extensive metabolizers (EM) have high to normal metabolic activity. Poor metabolizers (PM) are individuals who have low to absent metabolic activity. As there is lower metabolic clearance in these individuals, toxicity may result from medications that are normally metabolized by the isoenzymes. Intermediate metabolizers (IM) also have impaired or slow metabolic function that is greater than PMs, but less than EMs. The ultra rapid metabolizers (UM) have extreme metabolic activity leading to therapeutic failure. These metabolic phenotypes are closely related to gene coding for drug metabolizing enzymes. For CYP2D6 enzymes there are seventy variant alleles.

Asian patients respond to lower doses of some psychotropic drugs and are more likely to develop side effects. This issue is relevant to the effects of genetic polymorphism in the CYP2D6 system. Genetics and environmental factors are determinants of inter-individual and intraethnic variability in drug metabolism through the CYP2D6 system. For example, 6 percent of Caucasians have inactive CYP2D6 status. DNA-based tests can be used to see CYP2D6 status and prevent known side effects. About 15–30 percent of Asians are poor metabolizers of CYP2C19–affected drugs compared to 2–4 percent of Africans. While interactions between ziprasidone and risperidone are minimal and of no significance in most cases, the occasional addition of fluoxetine to risperidone therapy helps patients improve by increasing the level of risperidone.

CYP1A2. It is well established that clozapine is metabolized by CYP1A2. Fluoxamine, a selective serotonin uptake inhibitor, inhibits CYP1A2. Therefore, fluvoxamine causes 40–50 percent inhibition of clozapine clearance and, thereby, can cause clozapine toxicity. There is evidence that coffee may increase clozapine levels; also, cigarette smoking induces CYP1A2. After quitting smoking, enzyme induction of CYP1A2 is stopped and the metabolism of clozapine is slowed; therefore, with the same dosage of clozapine and with abrupt quitting of cigarette smoking, there can be an increase in clozapine levels leading to toxicity. Even seizures due to high levels of clozapine in these patients have been reported. Smoking cessation measures in these patients should also include a decrease in clozapine dosage.

Among ethnic minorities, such as Asians, Latinos, the Japanese, smoking is quite common. If smoking is stopped and the patient stabilized while in the hospital, the patient may return to smoking with the consequent induction of the enzyme CYP1A2. This enzyme induction decreases the blood level of clozapine, and, thus, the patient relapses again. The same holds true for olanzapine. There are many ethnic minority patients who relapse frequently because they return to smoking. Ethnic minority patients should be educated on the action of smoking vis-à-vis their drug blood levels. These patients should be carefully watched following discharge for a period of a few weeks; this should be done in case they go back to smoking and, thus, require an upward adjustment of their dose of olanzapine or clozapine. On the other hand, introduction of fluvoxamine may be beneficial while treating patients with small doses of clozapine, which results in less risk of side effects. Fluvoxamine, being an inhibitor of CYP1A2, can slow the metabolism of clozapine and, therefore, help to improve those who are rapid metabolizers. Inhibition or induction of the cytochrome P450 enzyme system could also happen, thus, leading to multiple drug interactions.

CYP2D6. In the case of CYP2D6, 5–10 percent of Caucasians and 1–2 percent of Asians are PMs. This leads to the erroneous impression that more Caucasians than Asians are PMs; thus requiring smaller doses of antipsychotic medications. Up to 50 percent of Asians carry a mutant allele CYP2D6*10, which is an intermediate functioning allele. Consequently, Asians constitute a high IM group, with possible impaired metabolic activity.

There is a consensus that CYP2D6 plays a role in the metabolism of clozapine. Such a role is supported by the finding that concurrent administration of paroxetine, an SSRI, increases the blood level of clozapine by CYP2D6 inhibition. It is reported that the concomitant administration of clozapine and the CYP2D6 substrate risperidone increases the clozapine level twofold, as both are CYP2D6 substrates. However, the clinical meaning of this finding is not definitive because the contributions of CYP2D6 are small. Clozapine is primarily metabolized by CYP3A4. Administration of nefazadone, an inhibitor of this enzyme, increases the blood level of clozapine.

CYP3A4. Both CYP2D6 and CYP3A4 metabolize risperidone. CYP1A2 metabolizes olanzapine. Therefore, fluvoxamine, an inhibitor of 1A4, increases the level of olanzapine by decreasing its metabolism. Cigarette smoking induces CYP1A4 and thereby decreases the level of olanzapine. This is particularly relevant for ethnic minority populations as African Americans, Asians, and Hispanics smoke frequently, and East Indians chew tobacco in addition to smoking. Similarly, concomitant administration of fluoxetine increases serum levels of olanzapine. Similar interactions are possible with quetiapine because it is also metabolized by CYP3A. Phenytoin decreases the levels of quetiapine, and ketoconozole increases its level. Among ethnic minority groups, variables such as age, weight, physical status, and hepatic/renal function cannot be disregarded. Drug interactions are related to cytochrome enzyme genotypes, and phenotype expressions can be modified by environmental factors.

CYP1A2

Antidepressants:	amitriptyline, clomipramine, imipramine, and fluvoxamine
Neuroleptics	haloperidol, phenothiazines, thiothixene, clozapine, and olanzapine
Others:	caffeine, theophylline, acetaminophen, and phenacetin

CYP2C19

Antidepressants:	imipramine, amitriptyline, clomipramine, and citalopram
Benzodiazepines:	diazepam
Others:	propranolol, hexobarbital, mephobarbital, proquanil, omeprazole, and s-mephenytoin

---

CYP2D6

Antidepressants:	amitriptyline, clomipramine, imipramine, desipramine, nortriptyline, trimipramine, fluoxetine, paroxetine, venlafaxine, and sertraline
Neuroleptics:	chlorpromazine, thioridazine, perphenazine, haloperidol, risperidone, clozapine, and sertindole
Others:	codeine, opiates, propranolol, and dextromethorphan

CYP3A4

Antidepressants:	mirtazapine, nefazodone, and sertraline
Neuroleptics:	thioridazine, haloperidol, clozapine, quetiapine, risperidone, sertindole, and ziprasidone
Mood stabilizers:	carbamazepine, gabapentin, and lamotrigine
Benzodiazepines:	alprazolam, clonazepam, diazepam, midazolam, triazolam, and zolpidem
Others:	diltiazem, nifedipine, verapamil, nimodipine, androgens, estrogens, cortisol, erythromycin, cyclosporin, lidocaine, codeine, and sildenafil

---

In summary, the most important human cytochrome P450 enzymes and their psychotropic substrates are as follows:

Based on ongoing literature reports (Note 7–3), the most accepted ethnopsychopharmacological information is as follows:

- Good response with lower dosages of tricyclics among Asians, Hispanics, and African Americans
- Higher side effects of tricyclics among Hispanics
- Good response to lower dosages of selective serotonin reuptake inhibitors (SSRIs) among African Americans
- Good response to lower dosages of typical neuroleptics among Asians and Hispanics

- Higher risk for tardive dyskinesia with the use of typical neuroleptics among African Americans
- Higher prolactin response with the use of atypical neuroleptics among Asians
- Good response with the use of lower dosages of lithium among Asians (Chinese, Japanese, etc.)
- Good response to lower dosages of atypical neuroleptics among Asians, including clozapine (especially among Koreans) and olanzapine, and among Hispanics, with risperidone in particular
- Good response to lower dosages of benzodiazepines among Asians

It is important however that further research efforts continue in this very important area.

PSYCHOPHARMACOLOGIC TREATMENT OF ETHNIC POPULATIONS

The emerging field of ethnopsychopharmacology has become a focus of considerable attention. While psychotropic drugs are generally effective in all population groups, cross-ethnic variations in treatment responses have been documented. Ethno-specific polymorphisms in genes governing pharmacokinetic and pharmacodynamic aspects of psychotropic drugs have been identified and may explain some of these variations. However, many other factors could, either directly or indirectly, be equally responsible. For example, diet and nutritional status, body mass, use and abuse of substances such as alcohol and cannabis, accessibility of health services, medication, treatment, compliance, social support, and comorbid medical conditions are all known to have an impact on the pharmacokinetics and pharmacodynamics of psychotropic drugs, and may differ markedly between ethnic groups.

Treatment of ethnic minorities involves both genetic and nongenetic factors. Genetic factors influence both the pharmacokinetics as well as the pharmacodynamics. The genotype determines the phenotypes. However, the boundaries between genotype and phenotype, and environmental factors are not clear. For instance, Scandinavians have a high incidence of prostate cancer, but after immigration to the United States, their prostate cancer rate becomes similar to that observed in the United States male population. The rate of breast cancer among Japanese women in Japan is low, but after arrival in the United States, the level gradually goes up, thus, indicating that there can be an interaction between phenotype and environmental factors.

Even within a cultural group, age, gender, food habits, smoking, and physical health all have profound influence. For instance, Sudanese persons metabolize antipyrine slowly, but Sudanese persons who have lived in the United Kingdom for years metabolize antipyrine similarly to the Caucasian population of the United Kingdom. Similarly, Indians in the United Kingdom who maintain a lacto-vegetarian diet have a pharmacokinetic profile similar to those in India, but those who become meat eaters were indistinguishable from Caucasian Britons. Some Chinese persons can be poor metabolizers of one antipsychotic drug, but may not show the same trait with another antipsychotic drug. This indicates yet another genetic variable not yet well identified.

PHARMACODYNAMICS

Among African Americans, smaller dosages of beta blockers are needed to improve hypertension. This is explained by the fact that African Americans have a higher level of lymphocyte-derived cyclic AMP, thus indicating a higher degree of b-adrenergic receptor activity. Six polymorphisms located in the serotonin 2A and 2C receptors, as well as transporter genes, predicted clozapine response in 77 percent of patients. A number of studies have shown a poor response to SSRIs in the presence of functional polymorphism in serotonin transporter genes. Pharmacokinetic variation with lithium has also been demonstrated. African Americans have a less efficient RBC lithium-sodium countertransport pathway. This observation is significant because the issue of neurotoxicity has remained a major concern in the management of African-American patients treated with lithium. A study has revealed that the blood lithium levels were identical in both African-American and Caucasian control subjects. However, twenty-five hours after lithium administration, lithium levels were higher among African-American populations than among Caucasian populations.

Many pharmacological agents are relatively nonpolar and require two metabolic steps. Step 1 metabolism consists of oxidation, reduction or hydrolysis to make the metabolite hydrophilic. Step 2 metabolism is involved in inactivation of the medication by coupling with glucuronic acid, glycine, glutathione, glutamate, or conjugation with sulfate, acetate, or methyl groups; thereby, facilitating renal excretion. None of the atypical antipsychotic drugs have significant variance in step 2 metabolism.

ALPHA GLYCOPROTEIN

Psychoactive drugs are lipophilic. Therefore, they have to rely on plasma proteins for their transportation into the cells. Variations in the concentration of these drug-binding proteins can significantly influence the effects of the drugs by changing the free fraction and thus, the amount of the unbound drug concentrations in plasma. Because of this unbound free drug, which can cross the blood brain barrier, plasma proteins have profound clinical significance.

CONCLUSIONS ON PSYCHOPHARMOGENETICS AND MINORITIES

There are genetic differences between ethnic groups that profoundly alter their drug response and the occurrence of side effects. While we relied primarily on the phenotype determination by using mephytoin or debrisoquine metabolism in the past, currently genotype assays are possible. In conclusion:

a) Genotype and phenotype examinations have revealed that 50 percent of Asians are slow metabolizers, and, therefore, they should be started with a low dose and watched carefully for the occurrence of side effects.

b) Tardive dyskinesia is more common among African Americans, and yet they frequently receive higher doses of neuroleptics. Traditional antipsychotic drugs should be, if at all possible, avoided. Each patient should be carefully monitored for signs of tardive dyskinesia.

c) The combination of antipsychotics and selective serotonin re-uptake inhibitors should be avoided or given with caution as this combination can increase antipsychotic levels and produce severe side effects. Such a combination, however, can be used with therapeutic advantage among rapid metabolizers.

d) Clozapine and fluvoxamine combination can produce clozapine toxicity as fluvoxamine is an inhibitor of 1A2 and 3A4 enzymes, and clozapine is metabolized by the same enzymes.

e) Nongenetic factors involved in treating ethnic minority patients should be kept in mind. Minority patients are more likely to avoid medications or take them in lower doses than prescribed.

Both genetic factors and nongenetic factors should guide the choice of the drug dosage and drug combinations. Side-effect profiles and risk of adverse effects of ethnic minorities, however, has to be considered when pharmacologically treating these patients.

CLINICIAN ATTITUDES

Elmira

The medical record would suggest that Elmira had been sick from the time her parents abruptly left Guatemala when Elmira was fifteen years of age. Going across Mexico with a number of friends was a major ordeal. They had opted for jumping into and out of trains when the trains were already moving or about to stop. Several friends were crushed. Others died in the Mojave desert when they were abandoned by a "coyote" guide. Both Elmira's mother and her older sister were assaulted and beaten by desert bandits. Elmira's father sustained major injuries from which he almost died. The family eventually made it to Santa Ana, California, where distant relatives assumed the family's care.

Elmira intermittently experienced palpitations, chest pain, shortness of breath, and feelings of impending doom. She had persistent nightmares about the events of her trip into the United States. The relatives' physician, who diagnosed asthma and briefly treated Elmira with medications that increased her symptoms, followed her at irregular intervals. A neighbor prescribed herbs that helped Elmira sleep, though her symptoms continued.

Elmira graduated from high school, went to junior college, and started working as a secretary. During college and in the ensuing years, Elmira had fluctuations in weight and appetite, long periods in which she lacked energy, had trouble thinking and concentrating, and had occasional ideas of death. She was diagnosed as having anemia, undernourishment, chronic fatigue syndrome, and recurrent bouts of bronchitis.

Shortly after she was married at age twenty-five, her husband, a successful computer programmer, also from Central America, insisted that she see a psychiatrist. His reason was that his mother had gone through similar experiences and similar symptoms, had received the diagnosis of depression, and had been doing well for years after treatment.

When we saw Elmira at the clinic, we were satisfied that all her symptoms could be explained by an initial post-traumatic syndrome, followed by major depression with secondary anxiety. She responded well to treatment with psychotherapy and antidepressants. She has been thankful that her response to treatment supported our conclusion that she probably hadn't had the multiple diseases diagnosed through the years.

For a very long time, we have had the benefit of reviewing the psychiatric records of minority patients at hospitals and clinics. When we have focused exclusively on patients who have received treatment for many years without a definite diagnosis, what first becomes obvious is that symptoms of anxiety and depression are repeatedly mentioned, but these diagnoses are not explored.

There is a growing body of research showing that minority patients are often misdiagnosed and that errors in diagnosis can be attributed more to clinician bias than to the patient's symptoms. Any effort at reducing the social, cultural, and attitudinal distance between the therapist and the patient will benefit not only the patient but also the whole community.

ADHERENCE

Daniel, Julieta, and Flora

Daniel has been our patient intermittently now for twenty-five years. The facts of his disorder have been clear all along: Daniel has schizoaffective disorder that produces episodes of hyperactivity, impulsive behavior, delusions, hallucinations, and bizarre behavior. Daniel usually waits until the police bring him to our facility, and then he is very compliant for days, or weeks. He responds well to lithium and risperidone, and usually goes back to normal behavior within two weeks. He claims he has learned his lesson and promises compliance and keeps a few out-patient appointments; but then he disappears for months, seldom for longer than one year, until the next episode.

Julieta is the opposite. She insists on taking 50 mg of nortriptyline every night, as she has for twenty years. As a young person, she suffered severe, chronic headaches, numerous body pains, much anxiety, and persistent depression. She tried to kill herself three times. She also underwent many hours of psychotherapy that did not help much. Since starting the medication, Julieta has considered herself free of symptoms and has functioned quite well as a wife, mother, interior decorator, and community leader in Mexico City. She says treatment was essential to her well-being. She visits our office in San Diego once a year.

Flora is somewhere in between. She came to the office on an emergency basis for the first time four years ago while suffering a severe depression. Though entertaining ideas of suicide, she was willing to commit to not killing herself. We agreed to see her daily during the first week. Then she came once a week for one month, but then refused to come back because she felt she was well. We had placed her on paroxetine the first day, and eventually assumed that she had stopped the medication on her own. Two years later she again came in on an emergency basis. She told us she had been taking paroxetine all along, thanks to prescriptions written by her family physician, who progressively reduced the dosage to 5 mg every second day. Flora was again depressed and requested a change of medication. We decided to try a larger dose of paroxetine, and Flora improved again. She failed to keep her third appointment.

When she returned to care at a later point, she had decreased the medication on her own and was again depressed. Our last discussion with her was about compliance and also about the use of mood stabilizers to prevent a new recurrence of depression.

IDEAL CONDITIONS FOR COMPLIANCE

The ideal conditions for compliance have been described many times. Below is a summary:

The patient is interested and motivated. The presence of symptoms produces interest in taking medications on the part of the patient and the family. The promise of a better and more successful life is a motivating factor for adherence to treatment. Among minorities, as among others, compliance is enhanced by the realization that the illness is a major obstacle to the fulfillment of hopes and goals.

The patient understands the reasons, conditions, and expected results of treatment. There are several matters about psychotropics that should be discussed with the patient: our ideas about the drug's mechanism of action, the potential side effects, and the expected latency period until therapeutic action starts (for SSRIs, one has to mention that the patient may first experience the side effects, and only later, or much later, the therapeutic effects).

The family understands and supports the treatment. We have repeatedly mentioned in this book that cooperation by the family is critical to the patient's success .

The patient and the family understand circumstances beyond the power of the psychiatrist. Physicians and patients have to deal with impositions by insurance companies, including limitations in duration and frequency of therapy, and the use of formularies. Our advice to our colleagues is that we have to take a position of principled resistance to any measure that interferes with treatment. Insurers and employers listen to our patients, and regulatory agencies are increasingly more receptive to our calls for action.

EXPECTATIONS

Ricardo

Ricardo repeatedly told us he was born with a dark cloud hanging above him. He was born to a Dominican mother and an African-American father in Harlem. His delivery was complicated, and he suffered hypoxia. As a child he had two convulsive seizures. After being placed on anticonvulsants, he did not have any more seizures. The medications were removed when he was about to enter kindergarten. Ricardo did poorly in primary school. Subsequently, he went to special education classes: "They were the morons. They never gave me a chance. They placed me with the worst kids ever." By age sixteen, Ricardo was known to be truant, escaped from home several times, and ended up in a gang. A burglary landed him in juvenile hall. When released at age eighteen, he rejoined his gang.

After a confrontation with another gang, in which several deaths resulted, Ricardo went to prison. He claims he was repeatedly raped there. When he went home after eight years, he was HIV positive, and soon developed Kaposi's sarcoma.

Ricardo's response to treatment was excellent. When we met him, he was free of symptoms, was an AIDS activist, ran socialization groups for families of AIDS patients, and helped run The Pantry, a meal service for HIV-positive patients.

As the years went on, Ricardo suffered damage to his face muscles, which gave him a bloated appearance. He gained weight, his cholesterol, blood sugar, and blood pressure became too high, and finally he developed a typical depressive syndrome.

Ricardo was highly skeptical about his need for psychiatric care: "You must be kidding. Just because I have had all the other diseases, you want me to believe I also have a depression? From the beginning I was chosen to die young, and now I have all I need to die young."

Ricardo belongs to a large and growing number of patients who have chronic or debilitating medical conditions, and often face a number of different diagnoses. These patients are increasingly coming to the attention of psychiatrists because of anxiety, depression, confused thinking, and plain despair about increasing symptoms, reduced financial ability, and mounting family problems.

Nineteen major cancer centers, along with the American Cancer Society, came together early in 2005 to formulate a screening test that includes ratings for the manifestations mentioned above. A high score indicates the need for intervention. Ricardo, for example, could readily accept that his vision of his own future was obscured by anxiety, pessimism, large bills, limited income, and lack of support from others. He was eventually willing to commit to treatment, on the basis that he couldn't help others if he was neglecting himself.

According to the World Health Organization, only around 50 percent of people comply with prescriptions from their doctors. Those who don't comply mention reasons such as forgetfulness, fear of side effects, confusion about prescriptions, and similar factors. We respond by persistently presenting explanations about the disorder, the treatment, and reasons to expect a better outcome.

RESISTANCE

That patients do not respond to medications has been frequently mentioned in these pages. In situations like those faced by Olo, who initially failed to respond to risperidone, common assumptions are that the patient is not compliant or is using drugs or herbs that may interfere with metabolism. Olo's therapist was finally satisfied that neither was the case. This is a challenge not only for patients on antipsychotics but those on other psychotropic medications as well. Only a minority of patients started on a new antidepressant are taking it after three months. Many patients go on to other antidepressants or augment them with mood stabilizers or other compounds. Many patients on antipsychotic medications take several of them, often accompanied by yet more medications for other disease states. Assuming full compliance, the current history of treatment with either antidepressants or antipsychotics, or both, indicates that partial or complete biologic resistance to one or several psychotropic medications is common.

THE PATIENT

Psychopharmacology is a rapidly changing amd developing field. We do expect that new discoveries will permit very targeted and individualized medication treatments. In the meantime, we have to take every precaution to assure that a given patient is likely to succeed while receiving psychotropic drugs.

Though much has been written about the psychiatric indications for drug therapy, less has been discussed about the medical evaluation of the patient about to receive treatment. The physician may forestall future problems if he knows the patient's vital signs, weight, height, body mass index, blood sugar, cholesterol, triglycerides, creatinine, liver enzymes, and thyroid hormones at the inception of treatment. This baseline information may be priceless when evaluating side effects that may occur later in the treatment.

Review of symptoms is very often helpful and sometimes produces surprises. We have found that patients who complain about blurred vision during treatment with psychotropics may have had the same problem while not taking medications. The same may happen for dry mouth. Approximately 10 percent of patients who want psychotherapy may be deaf. (Note 7–4). Cardiovascular manifestations suggestive of heart or lung conditions often are produced by anxiety. Gastrointestinal distress may exist much before the use of medications that may produce it. This is the case in patients with gastroesophageal reflux who may later complain of nausea and vomiting while on antidepressants. Sexual dysfunction is not uncommon among psychiatric patients before they take any medication. Being aware of any history of tremors, rigidity, restlessness, and seizures is of great importance when treating patients with many psychotropics.

FINAL WORDS

Psychopharmacology is advancing towards becoming a science, but is still largely an art. When prescribing for minority patients, following the best rules for optimal medical care is even more important (Note 7–5):

- Give the lowest effective dose for the shortest adequate time, always knowing that many patients will need to be maintained on medications.
- Avoid the large doses that come from thinking that more is better.

- Therapy should be tailored to all the information that is known about the patient and the potential side effects and adverse effects of the medication.
- The ultimate goal is to offer help without hurting the patient.

CHAPTER EIGHT

ODYSSEYS

THE HMONG

The explosion destroyed the American businessman's home. No, the attempt at killing his whole family was not orchestrated by Al-Qaeda. The legislator's father, a famous general, and others, had reasons to believe that different sinister forces were at work. The famous general had commanded the Hmong guerrillas who had fought the communists in Laos for several years in the 1960s. Many had reason to believe that the potential assassins had received orders from Laos.

The Hmong fled from China to Laos 200 years ago, after some 4,000 years of limited life as an unwelcome minority. Until the 1950s, there were no written communications in the Hmong language. In the 1960s, living close to the strategically located Ho Chi Minh Trail, the Hmong became critical allies of the American armed forces in the area. The Hmong soldiers became an army of as many as 30,000 soldiers. They paid dearly. During the war, some 20,000 Hmong soldiers died. When the communist forces arrived after the American withdrawal, the Hmong were killed or chased into the jungles or into neighboring Cambodia. Many came to the United States, where today they may number around 200,000 people.

Initially, not much was expected of the Hmong people in the United States. The officer of the Federal Office of Refugee Settlement in charge of overseeing the Hmong resettlement in the 1980s said, "When they arrived here, the Hmong were the least westernized, most unprepared for life in the United States of all the Southeast Asian refugee groups." Also in the 1980s, there was the statement by the U.S. Senator who said the Hmong were virtually incapable of integrating into American culture: "the most indigestible group in society."

When the first Hmong families arrived in the United States, their plight was compounded by their tendency to have large families and the U.S. resettlement policy that required refugees to be dispersed throughout the nation.

The Hmong Miracle

As mentioned, there are some 200,000 Hmong people in the United States today. They are not equally distributed and have done best in places like Minnesota, where 60,000 live. There they can best show the results of mutual support. The twin cities are called the Hmong capital of the world. There and elsewhere, the Hmong community now includes scores of physicians, lawyers, university professors, writers, poets, businessmen, and political leaders. An example is Mee Moua, who was born in a mountain village in Laos in 1969 and is now a state senator in Minnesota. She graduated from Brown University and obtained a law degree from the University of Minnesota (Note 8–1).

What about the destruction we mentioned? The victim of the bombing, Mr. Cha Vang, a successful businessman and community leader, may have been targeted because General Vang Pao, an undisputed leader of the Hmong community in the U.S., has advocated normal relations with the current government in Laos, which also happens to be the position of the U.S. Department of State, a position not necessarily popular with everyone.

Talking about relationships with another country and reactions among the people affected, let's look at another group of recent migrants to the United States.

THE CUBAN-AMERICANS

Americans born in Cuba thrived in the U.S. for many years before the 1959 Cuban revolution. Cuban scholars identify several waves of migration following early events in the Castro government. We are going to refer here only to recent migrants, whose feelings and ideas are relevant to our attempt to understand American odysseys. Our concept is based on findings of the Institute for Cuban and Cuban-American Studies (Note 8–2).

The study included a sample of Cuban émigrés eighteen years old or older. The 171 participants were approached while they were receiving orientation to life in the U.S. at the offices of the Church of World Services, one of two religious organizations aiding recently arrived Cubans in Miami. Of those participants surveyed, 76 percent described themselves as Caucasian, 60 percent had children, and 35 percent had migrated to U.S. with their spouses. As might be expected, in Cuba, they lived mostly in urban areas, most considered their homes acceptable, most had received money from abroad, most did not have their own transportation, and the largest majority (83 percent) rated Cuban urban transportation as poor. Ninety-six percent were in favor of a free market economy. Forty-one percent thought they belonged to the middle or upper class, the inference being that the remaining 59 percent felt they had been born to a family of very limited means.

They were an educated population: 91 percent had a high school degree, 46 percent had obtained technical or vocational training, and 9 percent had a university degree. As a group, they seem to have done well in Cuba, so that 18 percent had obtained professional or administrative positions, 39 percent technical or blue-collar positions, and 13 percent were self-employed. Eighty-two percent thought the Cuban educational system was good or average, and 96 percent would not change it. Eighty-one percent felt the Cuban medical system was good or average, and 94 percent would not change it. Seventy-one percent wanted Cuba to become a democracy, 90 percent wanted the reunification of all Cubans, 87 percent wanted improvement of the relationships between the U.S. and Cuba, and 85 percent wanted free elections.

Seventy percent of this group of recent émigrés favored the return of Cuban exiles, but a similar percentage, 74%, said they themselves would not return to Cuba. When asked about the three most difficult issues in Cuba, they mentioned being unable to express their true thoughts and opinions (78 percent), having limited options for the future (52 percent), and the lack of food and other essentials (50 percent). When asked about their own future and that of their children, it was clear that the group was future-oriented and willing to work hard in order to advance.

Our reading of this study suggested that the recent migrants are not very different from their predecessors, even in cases when they are separated by many years. Given their values, education, and willingness to work, they seemed destined to succeed.

As we will see in this chapter, the American odyssey of each group often includes a process of rapid growth once the right opportunities emerge. The oldest groups, including Native Americans and African Americans, often faced circumstances that robbed them of opportunity. Other groups may have had rapid growth because the opportunities were more readily available.

THE PASTOR

It took Dr. Charles E. Becknell a number of years to decide to write about himself. As he put it, "I realized that even though I had once been a public figure, I guarded my privacy to the point that when I felt my privacy being invaded, I became very defensive. However, with this book, my privacy is not being invaded; I am inviting others into my private world." (Note 8–3).

We became aware of Dr. Becknell's book through a dear friend, a very successful senior executive who had achieved prominent positions quite rapidly, before she had a stroke. She had spent her childhood in the black section of the then segregated town of Hobbs, New Mexico. When we expressed our admiration for her life achievements, she said, "Wait until you read about my classmate, Dr. Becknell."

Dr. Becknell had traced his family back to the biracial marriage of William Becknell and Mary Cribbs, in Missouri, in 1817. The Becknells had three children. In 1835, the Becknells moved to Red River County, Texas. There the family prospered. Mr. Becknell became a wealthy landowner, and preserved his fortune until his death in 1858.

Six generations after William, Charles was born in 1941. Eighteen months afterwards, his mother moved with Charles and his sister to Hobbs, in southeastern New Mexico.

Though Charles doesn't say so in his biography, it is pretty clear that he was a precocious child who soon realized that there were problems: "I grew up with the assumption that to be black and different was to be inferior. I also grew up believing that to be black was a badge of dishonor and that it equaled second-class citizenship. Second–class citizenship meant that you were to say *Yes sir* and *No sir* to white males, regardless of their age. Another rule that I learned at an early age was that blacks had to remove their caps or hats in the presence of a white person. Black men and boys, regardless of age, were frequently referred to as *boy.*"

Just in case that there was any doubt, the radio images of Amos and Andy, and the bumbling screen image of Stepin Fetchit reinforced the opinion many had of the black American. "The negative impact of racism, separation and rejection could be seen in the actions of those blacks who bleached their skin in efforts to have light skin like white people," wrote Dr. Becknell.

**Dr. Becknell's first chapter, "The Torn Page,"
has the following story:**

I vividly remember that when I received my first-grade book, one of
the pages was torn. I asked Ms. Porter, "Why is my book torn?"

She replied, "These books are sent to us after the white children finish with them."

Many years later, Dr. Becknell would write: "Racial scars cut
deep and bleed profusely. Although the bleeding eventually stops,
the scars remain as reminders of the pain. At some time you learn to
move on, try to ignore those scars, but each act of racism creates a
new scar, and unfortunately the old ones remain."

Until 1954 the school system and the communities in Hobbs
were totally segregated. Everyone at Charles's school was black, and,
as he could show later, the facilities, the budgets, and the opportunities were inferior. However, the teachers, the real community advocates, were excellent.

The landmark decision of the Supreme Court in *Brown* v. *Board
of Education* effectively ended segregation in 1954. Hobbs was the
last school district in New Mexico to end segregation in its schools.

The fall of 1954 marked the beginning of a new and different life
for Charles. Integration of the school system had not ended discrimination and, at times, made life more difficult. When three white students attacked Charles with no provocation, he was the only one
punished. There was only one black teacher in the school.

One gathers from Dr. Becknell's narrative that he had developed
into an exceptional athlete who excelled in all sports, especially football. The basketball coach was a fair man who understood Charles
and helped him become ever better. The football coach was a very
narrow man with no experience coaching black athletes, but with a
great hatred for them. After Charles had scored a spectacular touch-

down, the coach failed to recognize his achievement, but punished him for having caught the ball with one hand. That was the end of his football career. He was not a swimmer or a skier because he had never had the opportunity to learn swimming or skiing. He continued to excel in basketball. Even with his clear talents, Charles might have had a hard time making it out of Hobbs after high school had the basketball coach from St. Joseph's College (Albuquerque, NM) not seen him play, and immediately approached him with an invitation to come to St. Joseph's.

As a teenager, Charles already had very strong values: "I grew up developing a strong sense of justice and fairness. I later developed the attitude that racism must be confronted, no matter where it comes from and whenever it rears its ugly head."

In college, in a multicultural, multiethnic and multireligious environment, Charles thrived. Again he showed his outstanding intellectual and physical qualities, and made many friends, more than a few for life. In May 1964, he obtained his bachelor of science degree in education.

The ensuing ten years were far from easy, but in retrospect seem to have been a succession of victories. Becknell received a Ford Foundation Fellowship under the Leadership Development program, served an internship at Duke University, and went on to doctoral studies at Columbia University. In May, 1975, he received his Ph.D. from the University of New Mexico, where he had founded and directed the African-American Studies Program.

During Jerry Apodaca's term as governor of New Mexico, he appointed Dr. Becknell to several senior administrative positions. After a reorganization of the state administrative departments, Dr. Becknell became secretary of the Department of Criminal Justice. This assignment placed the state police and the correctional facilities under his control. Dr. Becknell's recollections show that he was a competent administrator, even though he couldn't prevent the results of unjustified attacks from several quarters. Jerry Apodaca was a fair player, and Dr. Becknell felt supported in all his tough decisions. The same couldn't be said about Jerry's successor, and soon Dr. Becknell found himself feeling betrayed and, shortly thereafter, unemployed. Years later the situation repeated itself when the mayor of Albuquerque asked Dr. Becknell to organize and direct the Department of General Services for the city. After a short tenure, he was asked to be the director of Personnel. His tenure was again short; he was terminated because he refused to follow a direct order he didn't consider fair.

Dr. Becknell later became well known as a writer, poet, lecturer, and an expert in training and human development. He has been the pastor of two churches and has led his own consulting firm for a number of years.

If we understand Dr. Becknell's odyssey, we may understand those of others who started with little, faced seemingly insurmountable obstacles, took on those who attacked them, and could later show a life full of accomplishments.

THE NATIVE AMERICANS

Just as we view the Hmong as among the most recent groups to join the American experience, we may view Native Americans as those who have been part of it all along. (Note 8–4).

A 2003 Commission on Civil Rights report indicated that Native Americans continued to suffer a quiet crisis of discrimination, poverty, and unmet promises. And yet, even in the midst of poor education, high crime, lack of jobs, lack of opportunities, diabetes, cancer, and high rates of heart disease, the Native Americans, much before the report, and after having been driven almost into extinction, were starting to see the fruits of self-determination, new opportunities for education, and new tribal businesses.

By 1920, Native Americans numbered only 350,000 people. Today, 2.5 million Americans report themselves as having only Native-American blood, and over 4 million say they are Native Americans. In this population, the median family income is going up, more people are going on to postgraduate education, and the infant mortality rate is going down.

There are now 562 tribes recognized by the federal government. Native Americans now run casinos that have become a \$17 billion industry. The largest of these casinos is the Foxwoods Resort Casino, in Connecticut. It is owned by the 880–strong Mashantucket Pequot tribe, whose members trace their roots to the eleven individuals who lived on the reservation one hundred years ago. Casinos are not the only areas of progress on the reservations. The Confederate Tribes of Warm Springs, in Oregon, have also invested in business ventures, natural resources, and agriculture. The proceeds generated have gone to health and education, as well as to the purchase of new lands.

Today, 60 percent of Native Americans live away from the reservations, almost half in cities. California has 333,300, many of them in the Los Angeles area. Chicago has 30,000. The American Indian Center, a self-help agency started in 1953 that offers programs and cultural events for a community of Native Americans from more than 100 tribes, supports the native communiy.

There is a marked similarity between the psychiatric difficulties that afflict Native Americans and those identified in other minority groups. Alcoholism, drug dependence, depression, other psychiatric disorders, and suicide are problems that will continue to require heightened attention. As in other minority communities, lack of awareness and lack of professionals will continue to hamper Native Americans interested in obtaining better psychiatric services.

NUMBERS

A study of diversity and disparities in the U.S. requires an examination of the changes that different groups will undergo in the years to come. Because congressional and state representation, as well as electoral votes in presidential elections, apportioned according to population, demographic changes will determine future political power in the country. (Note 8–5).

The figures we will consider here are derived from census reports. In 1970, the Latino population was reported as slightly higher than 9 million or 4.4 percent of the total population. Between 1970 and 1980, the Latino population increased by over 61 percent to reach 14.6 million persons. Between 1980 and 1990, the Latino population increased by 53 percent to reach 22.4 million people. The 2000 census reported a population of 35.6 million, therefore the growth in the preceding decade was 57.9 percent.

Between 1990 and 2000, the minority population (Latinos, African Americans, Asian/Pacific Islanders, American Indian/Alaskan Natives, and multi-racials), rose to 57 percent of the population—a majority—in the nation's 100 largest cities.

Migration has contributed greatly to the growing number of Latinos in the United States. In 1960, 9 percent of the foreign-born population in the United States had come from Latin America. By 2002 this figure had changed to 52.2 percent. In 1970 only 16 percent of the Latino population in the United States was foreign-born. In 2002 this figure had increased to 40.2 percent.

We started this section on numbers with a statement about the need minorities have to acquire and use political power. How are they doing? After thinking of a number of key indicators, we decided for one: The election of members to the U.S. House of Representatives. Let's look at several states where minorities are wielding increasing power.

New York

Minorities have been making steady progress in New York. As in states where the African-American community has been creating strong roots, Latinos have also settled in the common areas, often creating effective coalitions. In New York there have been powerful African-American congressmen who represent districts with large Latino populations. Congressman Charles Rangel, a very forceful minority advocate, represents District 15, with a population 30.5 percent African American and 47.9 percent Latino. In some cases, a minority congressman represents a district with limited minority population. Congressman Steve Israel represents District 2, that is 9.8 percent African American and 13.9 percent Latino.

Five out of 29 representatives (2 African American and 2 Latinos) are minority members of the House from New York.

Illinois

African-American and Latino groups have been making steady progress in Illinois for several decades. In the view of many, a pivotal event was Harold Washington's historic mayoral election in 1983, when Latino voters provided the margin of victory. He received 74 percent of the Latino vote.

The coalescence of minorities in the 1980s is more striking when it is understood as the collaboration of groups that came from very different geographic origins. The Latinos were from Puerto Rico, Cuba, Dominican Republic, and South America. In 1982 the Mexican American Legal Defense and Educational Fund had sued the city of Chicago, claiming discrimination of district apportionment. By 1986 three Latino eldermen had been elected.

Four out of 19 representatives (3 African American and 1 Latino) are minority members of the House from Illinois. Of note, 74.4 percent of the people in Jesse Jackson, Jr.'s District, 2 are minorities.

Georgia

Our perception is that coalitions similar to those in New York and Illinois will emerge, mainly in cities with large Latino populations like Chamblee (56 percent), Gainesville (33 percent), and North Atlanta (27 percent). For the time being, the congressional delegation represents the problems that minorities may have to surmount.

Three out of 13 representatives (all African American) are minority members of the House from Georgia. Two districts with black population majorities have black representatives to the House. Another district with a 49.7 percent population of minorities (44.5 percent African American) also has a minority representative. Several other districts are approaching a substantial minority presence.

Florida

The first minority member to serve in the U.S. Congress was Joseph Marion Hernandez, from St. Augustine, who served from 1821 to 1822, 167 years before another Latino came from Florida to serve in Congress.

The Latino population grew from 1,547,143 in 1990 to 2,682,715 in 2000, an increase of 70 percent. Today the total minority population of Florida is 34.5 percent (14.1 percent African American and 16.7 percent Latino). Latinos are a majority in several cities: Miami, Hialeah, Fountainebleau, Tamiami, Miami Beach, and Kendale Lakes.

Six out of 25 representatives (3 African American and 3 Latinos) are minority members of the House from Florida.

Texas

The history of Latinos in Texas started with the Spanish settlements of the eighteenth century. After Mexico obtained independence in 1821, Texas briefly belonged to the Mexican republic, but became an independent nation in 1836. In 1845 it became part of the United States.

Many African Americans came to Texas, starting late in the first half of the nineteenth century. Their numbers are uncertain because black descendants of white families were not properly recorded.

Latinos also became mostly poor, disenfranchised, and under-represented. Blacks and Latinos have made progress in the last decades, but the results are, so far, less than expected, and minority advocates still face strong opposition. As this book is being written, the courts are trying to decide on a congressional district distribution that may advance or paralyze the struggle towards fairness.

Eight out of 32 representatives (2 African Americans and 6 Latinos) are minority members of the House from Texas.

New Mexico

Spain had a presence in New Mexico long before the first Spanish settlements emerged in Texas. Santa Fe became the capital of the province in 1610. After New Mexico became a territory of the United States, between 1853 and 1923, ten Latinos served as delegates to Congress from the New Mexico Territory.

The history of Latinos and blacks in New Mexico has been characterized by many shifts. We have seen how Dr. Becknell was a high officer during the administration of Latino governor Jerry Apodaca, but was not welcome by his successor. The small percentage of the population that is black has suffered more because it is not as visible. (Note 8–6).

Statewide, minorities are 55.3 percent of the population. There are no minority representatives in the House from New Mexico. This situation deserves further explanation. Three Latinos from New Mexico have served in the U.S. Senate. Six Latinos from New Mexico have served in the House of Representatives. One of them, William B. Richardson, the current governor of New Mexico, is one of the most prominent Latino leaders in the country. In each of the three congressional districts, minorites make up the majority percentage; statewide, 55.3 percent of the population is minorities. To us it is clear that the time for better minority organization has arrived.

California

In 1542, Juan Rodriguez de Cabrillo founded San Diego—with the name of San Miguel, and initiated the Spanish exploration of the Pacific coastal areas. In 1769, Franciscan monks started establishing the missions that are today the largest cities in California. Mexico ceded California to the U.S. after the Mexican-American War of 1846–1848. Attracted by the prospect of immense gold fortunes, large numbers of Americans came to California in 1848, so that the territory qualified as a new state in the Union in 1849. In 1877 Romualdo Pacheco, previously a California governor, was elected to the U.S. House of Representatives. After Mr. Pacheco finally left the House in 1883, no Latino from California was elected until 1962, when Edward Roybal initiated his thirty-year tenure in the House. In 1993 he was replaced by his daughter, Lucille Roybal-Allard.

All minority groups have grown in California. Though all are represented throughout the state, there is a substantial Asian presence in northern California, and a large Latino majority in southern California. It is said that Los Angeles is the home to more Native Americans than any reservation. African Americans have led the way to progress especially in Los Angeles, where their presence has been decisive in the progress of all groups. Minorities are a majority of the population in 30 out of 53 congressional districts, and constitute 53.3 percent of the statewide population.

Seven Latinos and 4 African Americans are currently in the U.S. House of Representatives from California. In a state in rapid transition, these figures are likely to change, and be enhanced by a growing Asian contingent.

THE FUTURE

New York, Illinois, Georgia, Florida, Texas, and California, have elected almost half of the Congressional Black Caucus and the majority of the Hispanic Americans currently serving in the U.S. House of Representatives.

The long tenure of many of these legislators and their ability to preserve their districts for successors from the same minority demonstrate that election to the U.S. House of Representatives from a district with a large minority population may be the best indicator of further progress. However, the history of New Mexico demonstrates that election to a high office without firm support from a large and committed group may not necessarily lead to political gains.

CHAPTER NINE

THE TEXTURE AND BEAUTY OF COLOR

The Role of the Family in Different Cultures

FAMILY AND COMMUNITY RELATIONSHIPS

The American culture is full of colors—white, black, brown, yellow, and others. It is like a multicolored quilt with each color having its own texture and beauty. The big metropolitan cities generally have a number of different groups providing a multiethnic population and ambience. Los Angeles, being near to the Asian countries and close to Mexico, has a huge population of Hispanics and Asians. Each ethnic group has brought its own unique culture with distinctive beliefs, values, and problem solving methods. The process of acculturation of the various ethnic groups has created several subgroups within each ethnic group. The most acculturated group includes people who are educated, fluent in the English language, and who follow Western traditions with ease. They tend to adapt to the United States majority culture without much distress. Another group is comprised of middle-class people who follow the values and beliefs of their original culture but are also acculturated to the new values of the majority culture to some degree. Another group is the true ethnic culture group, which consists of people who follow rigidly the values and beliefs of their own original culture. Even those who have adapted well to the United States majority culture fall back to the traditional values and beliefs in times of stress, such as marriage, the birth of a baby, sickness, and loss of a relative. The concepts of mental illness and its treatment often stem from normative social and cultural constructions. People may have various culturally shaped frameworks to explain their mental illness, which are all valid. Their sickness behavior, expectation of treatment methods, and outcomes differ according to their ethnicity and cultural background. Symptom manifestations can also depend on the culture of origin. The following case is an example of some of these unique problems and solutions.

Mahayana, a twenty-eight-year-old single male, who worked as an engineer, was living in a joint family comprised of his younger sister and mother. He was considered capable, and although somewhat isolated, well-liked by his fellow workers for his hard work and efficiency. He suddenly developed a psychosis without any detectable precipitating event. The psychosis was manifested by severe insomnia, seeing God, worrying that his life was in danger, and blunted affect. He prayed to God often, did not eat well, and did not care for himself. His family worried that he would wander away from home and was also concerned about his physical health, given his belief that food had something to do with his illness. The family brought him to the local emergency center, and the patient was admitted to the psychiatric unit on an involuntary basis, given the fact that he vehemently denied being mentally ill.

In the psychiatric unit, Mahayana was found to be isolative and did not mix with other patients. He worshipped God whenever he could and was passively cooperative in taking his medications and following the ward routines. The nurses liked him, but could not understand his behavior. During examinations, he was cooperative, but denied that he had mental illness. He admitted to hearing God's voice and seeing God. God was telling him to lead a "good" (moral) life. He felt that his past life (karma) was catching up with him. He felt the need to go home and take care of his mother and sister. Being a Hindu, he felt that he was shirking his responsibility of looking after his family by being in the hospital. He did not believe that he was mentally ill, and he asked, "If I were to be mentally ill, why would I hear God's voice?"

Family members accompanied Mahayana to the hospital on his first day and wanted to sit through the assessment interview. When the psychiatrist tried to discuss the confidentiality issues between the patient and his doctor, the sister remarked, "We are a family. We care for and help each other. Your confidentiality does not help my brother or feed him." The patient did not express any objection. So, the family sat through the assessment interview and participated freely. Family members visited him every day. He looked forward to the visits and was happy to see them. At times, he began to cry while talking to his mother.

Mahayana's family called the psychiatrist at home periodically to discuss issues pertaining to the patient, who responded poorly to the antipsychotic regimen. His visual hallucinations and paranoid delusions continued unabated, even after three weeks of adequate psychopharmacological treatment. At the end of the three weeks, his family took the patient out on a day pass. When he came back to the hospital, the family brought the psychiatrist fruits that were offered to worship God. They informed the psychiatrist that they went to visit their local priest and worshipped God. The priest had told them that the patient would do well in another two weeks if he were to take his prescribed medications. The patient did improve to the extent that he could go home in about two weeks following his visit to the religious temple. The entire family came to the psychiatrist's office to discuss Mahayana's discharge plans but did not want to talk to the social worker. The family was eager to take the patient home and to care for him. They were sure that he would go back to work as the priest had predicted. They asked the psychiatrist a number of questions, which included the psychiatrist's belief in God, the part of India he came from, and whether he lived with his family.

Every detail of the medication regimen was discussed, such as whether medications needed to be taken with or without food, what reactions to watch for, and how often Mahayana should come for follow-up visits. Twice a month follow-up visits were planned. At every visit, all the family members came together and freely discussed the patient's symptoms, behavior, medication, and improvement as well as the medication's side effects. Three months later, the patient improved to such a degree that he could go back to work.

This case highlights successful family involvement and their willingness to care for the patient, their reluctance to send him to a residential program, their willingness to go to the temple to worship, their obtaining help from the priest, and their concept of confidentiality.

FAMILY SYSTEM

The family is a complex institution that can be assessed and understood according to various dimensions, including individual members as the subsystem of the family, the intersectional pattern of the family as a group, the life cycle of the family, and the family as a whole system. It is necessary to cover these aspects in order to provide culturally relevant assessments and treatment. Society provides the means and goals that shape the personalities of the members of the family.

GENERAL FUNCTIONS

To ascertain general functions, the family can be divided into several groups. It is in the family that human beings live most of their lives. The family constitutes the most important group in relation to the individual's psychological functioning, emotional interaction, and maintenance of self-esteem. The family has a history and function of its own, which differs from that of its individual members and of the members of different ethnic groups. The family is also bound together by intense and long-lasting ties, past experiences, social roles, mutual support, needs, and expectations.

Asian Family

The Asian family is a source of strong identity for its members. Roles and positions of hierarchy are evident in traditional Asian families. Specifically, elders are placed in roles of authority, and men are considered to be higher in the hierarchy than women. The father is considered the leader and authority of the family, whereas the traditional mother is the primary caregiver to the children of the household. Children also have specific roles in the family and are expected to have unquestioning respect for parents, grandparents, and other family elders. In the absence of the father, the oldest son assumes the role of head of the family.

Gary, a forty-two-year-old male patient, regularly attended the outpatient department accompanied by his parents. For the past few months, he came alone to his appointments. The treatment team was concerned about the health of his aged parents. A social worker was sent to Gary's home to find out if the parents were doing well. The parents lived only two blocks from the hospital. After a home visit, the social worker reported that the parents were very old and unable to take care of Gary. It was then decided by the treatment team that the patient would be placed in a residential facility, so the parents could have some rest. The parents did not like the decision that they could not care for their son. A residential facility was available near Gary's home, and he was placed in that facility against the wishes of his parents.

A month later, Gary came for his follow-up appointment accompanied by his brother. During the interview, Gary told the psychiatrists that his parents did not like the idea of his living in a residential facility while his family members were alive. Therefore, his parents asked Gary and his brother to move into their home, so Gary could live with them and his brother could help care for him when necessary. The parents were called to find out why they were not cooperating with the treatment plan. The father said that he was "Japanese" and as long as he lived it was his duty to look after his son.

He was deeply hurt that his son was put into a residential facility. The psychiatrist apologized for unwittingly hurting his feelings. Even after several years, the patient still lives with his brother, who cares for him. The brother is not married and is not planning to get married as he has assumed responsibility for Gary in accordance with the wishes of his parents. This case illustrates how many psychiatrists treat patients according to the Western value system only to realize that such solutions are not acceptable to a traditional Asian family.

Attitude Towards Sexuality in Eastern Families

One of the traditional Asian cultural values is sexual chastity before marriage and faithfulness after marriage. This traditional expectation of faithfulness applies quite strictly to the wife. In general, sexuality is considered a taboo topic for discussion in Asian communities. These views about sexuality are important, given that sexual assaults have been identified as one of the three most severe forms of pre-migration traumas endured by women refugees from Southeast Asia. Without considering the individual's sociocultural background through beliefs and attitudes, trauma cannot be defined. Asian views regarding sexuality must be considered when obtaining a patient's sexual history and while examining the female Asian rape victim.

Women typically blame themselves for rape in Asian culture, and therefore they rarely seek help related to sexual assault. For them, rape is not only a personal violation that results in loss of self-respect, but it is also a form of dishonor to the family. Society's reaction to the individual's traumatic experience is related to the consequences of the trauma. Examples of social consequences of rape in Asian cultures include community rejection, family disownment, and divorce. In India, raped unwed mothers tend to commit suicide as they are always blamed for the rape. These negative social reactions can impact on the victim's ability to share her experiences, even with her psychiatrist. Thus, Asian women who have experienced sexual assaults may not reveal their sexual traumas due to the severe social and cultural implications and thus, may suffer in silence to maintain their secret from others.

Asian men and women, particularly Indians, do not wish to discuss their sexual life with psychiatrists. Sex is considered to be for procreation and not for pleasure. Psychiatrists have to wait patiently until the patients are willing to discuss their sexual problems.

Latino Family

Hispanics, in general, share certain cultural characteristics of the majority culture of the United States, but differ in some aspects. They manifest "familismo," the strong identification and attachment to the nuclear family and extended family. A familismo also contains a sense of loyalty and duty. Respect for elderly people and for those in positions of authority is an important aspect of Latino culture. In contrast to Caucasian Americans, a more traditional sense of gender roles, such as the ideal obedient woman, is prevalent among traditional Hispanic groups. The roles are hierarchically organized with paternal dominance. Males are the heads of the family. Females are generally housewives, and their virginity is safely guarded until marriage. The Latino family emphasizes the needs, objectives, and goals of the group as being more important than those of the individual family member. Family needs take precedence over the individual's needs. "The family" often refers to three-generation families, and not to the nuclear family. Decision making and emotional support are the roles of the extended family. Kinship is extended to the members outside of the family. The avoidance of direct anger and confrontation between people is followed strictly so that relationships can follow smoothly and nicely. Expression of emotions towards one's own family are limited by the cultural taboos, such as that one should not speak ill of one's husband or parents. Taking care of the elderly and the children and providing financial and emotional support to family members in the United States and their own country are traditional values.

There are traditional ways of preventing emotional turmoil, which may be completely lost as soon as the Latino immigrant is in the host country. Many members of the family who reside in the United States fail to completely relinquish the role of assisting or helping the sick. Family secrets are never to be told outside of the family. An abusive husband tends not to be reported, even after several years of abuse. This makes it difficult to elicit much-needed information to treat the patient properly. Appropriateness to cultural values and treatment expectations of the patient are also important. Talking openly against the family is very painful. Open expressions usually become moral issues that produce severe shame. Emotional turmoil as well as the traditional values may ultimately ruin family relationships, which is very important for the Hispanic minority patients.

Cambodian and Thai Families

Most Cambodian and Thai people follow Buddhism, a religion that encourages acceptance of losses, resignation to the suffering of life situations, little expectation for better times during one's lifetime, and dignified and moral behavior to ensure a better afterlife. Most Cambodian refugees do not complain about their situations or blame others their inability to adjust; also, they do not share their suffering with each other. Despite their difficulties, they work hard and try to express an optimistic attitude. Fatalism is the acceptance of one's situation. They view traumatic experiences within their Buddhist belief system, and therefore, life experiences are regarded as meaningful occurrences of fate, determined by actions, or Karma. Additionally, this fatalistic approach to one's present existence is also related to Buddhist teachings that a person controls his or her own destiny through free will and cannot escape present suffering in this world. These beliefs keep Buddhist families away from seeking help but may produce distress within the family. Even when a person seeks help, the distress of the person is not apparent, and the family does not convey its concerns, thus, creating a puzzling situation for the psychiatrist.

Psychiatrists need to be patient and must allow ample time for patients to discuss their Karma and its current effects. Over time, patients will still connect the present suffering to Karma. At that time, a window of opportunity can be utilized for the benefit of patients and their families.

Indian Family

South Asian Indian civilization is based on a very different philosophy. The norms and values of the Hindu family are based on Buddhism and Hinduism. There are many interesting concepts such as "It is better to do one's own duty badly than to do others' duty well," thus, indicating that the role of each Indian is rigid. The value "good is rewarded and evil is always punished" indicates that the roles are prescribed and the behavior to be displayed in different circumstances is clearly delineated. Indian society's hierarchical and social positions are invariably arranged in a superior-subordinate order. There are elaborately formalized rules and regulations assigned to each position, and people are required to conform to them. Indians have a tendency to regard their social positions as superior to some and subordinate to others. Thus, they develop a cognitive map of hierarchical relations, which they utilize in social interactions. For example, the roles of wife, husband, son, daughter, friend, boss, and servant are clear. Therefore, sameness is easy to maintain. This provides the stability required by the culture, but at the expense of dynamism.

Each person in this culture possesses the resources to influence others to maintain stability. Hindus believe in reincarnation. Depending on one's actions, or Karma, in this life and previous lives, the person may be born again as a human or an animal. Karma is related to deeds in the previous life. The fear of Karma catching up in the future life may also compel Indians to maintain rigid role behaviors.

Traditionally, Indians live in joint families in which three or more generations live under the same roof. This provides multiple role models for the developing child. Such multiple role models provide the child with multiple coping skills, including interdependence, sharing, and sacrifice. The primary mechanisms in controlling of adolescents are shame and a sense of moral obligation. The integration of the family is maintained through a deep-seated belief in social values and obligation to duty. Belief in the integrity of the group provides the family with group cohesion and strengthens family stability at the cost of individual autonomy. Age, gender, and generational status serve as the determinants of behavior and role relationships. For example, an uncle is respected even if he is younger than the nephew. A high premium is placed on conformity and interdependence, but self-identity is inhibited. Conservatism and resistance to change are rewarded. The fixed role leads to the development of a culturally engineered personality. A submissive son, not a creative one, is the most desirable. Conformity and not expression, as well as sacrifice and not self-achievement, are taught subtly and constantly. The traditions are often maintained by the rural population, the less educated, and the elderly. The longer the stay in the United States, the less traditional the immigrant becomes.

The traditional values and lifestyles of Indians can be summarized as follows: 1) Indians are allocentric and not idiocentric, and the individual is expected to make sacrifices for the good of the group and the family; 2) males are decision makers and disciplinarians; women are subordinate and act as caretakers responsible for cooking, cleaning, and sometimes, hard labor.

From the time of birth, women are groomed to take care of the well-being of the husband and the family. Generally, women are the carriers of the culture while the men are the breadwinners. The mother has some power in joint families. Most often she is assigned the role of keeping daughters, daughters-in-law, and grandchildren within the Indian cultural value system. The daughter-in-law has to be obedient to the in-laws, and this may create friction in some families.

Within the family and among the relatives, disagreements and conflicts are not verbalized. The daughter-in-law may be mistreated, and yet none in the family expresses disagreement openly. The family functions as a unit in the midst of unresolved situations. The cultural modes of coping with intrafamily conflicts are self-correction, information through mediation, and change in the father's behavior secondary to the unhappiness of the son. Confrontation is not the route to follow. There is constant goal-directed and uniform pressure to conform within the family. In Indian society, everything has a place and time, and everything is connected.

The family is held together by an intuitively shared symbiotic and empathic atmosphere. In such a situation, the sparking of any emotion would immediately spread. Therefore, emotions have to be carefully contained or expressed in a prescribed form, such as subtle gestures or shared expressions. Even outside the family, one tends to attach family labels to those with whom one has to deal in close quarters. For example, many friends and relatives become uncles and aunts.

The ego problems are collective. For example, a person is not terribly hurt when something happens to him, such as when the family is insulted by a sister-in-law, or is not respected by a relative or by the community. The reason for this is that the insult was directed to the entire community in general and to the family in particular, not to any individual member of the family. These problems are not solved by emotional expression, but by endurance. As the ego boundaries are not definitive, rigid external rules compensate for the fluidity of the ego. For appropriate functioning, family and community are needed. Traditional child rearing involves encouraging imitation and immediate control rather than stimulating introjections of values and pursuing long-term goals. What the child has to learn is his or her role in the successive, well-characterized phases of the life cycle and the socially approved behavior required by various situations. Role-play and context-oriented behavior are therefore more important than the formation of a cohesive, consistent personality core.

From such a personality, the behavior would flow in an individually predictable and socially conforming fashion. The models for such behavior are not contemporary, but the traditional characters from epic stories. Therefore, thinking becomes rigid. Individual history becomes less important than the traditional life of complete stages with all their rituals. Being able to play the expected role in one's limited social network assumes dominance. Personal points of view and fantasy are not at a high premium. The only degree of freedom for an individual is in the spiritual sphere.

African-American Family

The family life of the typical African-American is dominated by religion and spirituality. Worship, prayer meetings, and participation in leadership and administration of church activities provide a spiritual structure to the work week, as well as purpose and opportunities for recognition that may not be available in the workplace. The religious setting also provides support for child rearing and discipline in the context of religious teachings as well as an opportunity for fellowship, social support, and coping with stressful life events.

In African-American families with two parents, gender roles tend to be egalitarian, without the strict delegation to women of the chores of cooking and child care as in other cultural groups. Concepts of family, in African Americans, extend beyond the nuclear family to include the extended family of aunts, uncles, parents, and grandparents. The extended family may also include godparents, church members, and even fictive kin, those individuals who are not blood-related, but are regarded with closeness and referred to as if they were biologically related.

Given the high divorce rate among African Americans, there is a high proportion of families in which there is a single female head of household. These families may experience higher rates of poverty due to the mother being the only breadwinner. The grandmother plays an important role in these families, providing crucial support to the mother and grandchildren. Quite often, African Americans feel that society promises opportunities but does not deliver. The history of slavery, and ongoing experiences of racism and racial discrimination regardless of socioeconomic status have a major impact on employment, housing, economic and educational opportunities, and substandard health care. These realities create the backdrop for a suspicious attitude toward the larger society, including health institutions. In the face of symptoms of mental illness, professional help from mental health specialists is often not sought due to the extreme stigma associated with mental illness and the use of alternative sources of support, such as informal help from family, extended family, friends, and neighbors. Duration of untreated psychosis has been noted to be as long as one year in African-American families, and this finding does not correlate with family member's knowledge of mental illness. Early symptoms are often attributed to depression, lack of motivation, and contemporary environmental stressors. Until the symptoms become unbearable or disruptive, help is not sought. When help is sought, it may be more likely to be obtained from crisis or emergency settings.

Difficulty with access to care, stigma, reliance on religious support and extended family support contributes to the family's decision not to seek help early. In addition, family members may differ in their opinion on the presence of mental illness, its causes, its treatment, and how they could help the patient. Furthermore, cultural norms regarding maintaining privacy and the sanctity of family "business" is a major barrier to the type of disclosure that is expected in mental-health care settings. This finding makes it imperative that families be educated about mental illness, its causes, and important aspects of treatment. Also, treatment should involve as many members of the family as possible, so there is a concordance among family members about mental illness and their role in helping the patient. Active involvement, guidance, and concrete steps to help the patient and the family will provide the basis of an effective treatment. Spirituality is also a useful means of coping, and pastors and other religious leaders are often the first ones that families turn to for support in the face of adversity, crisis, or symptoms of mental illness. Educating African-American religious-community leaders about mental health and mental illness is one strategy for improving help-seeking and mental-health services utilization.

INTERPRETING THE CULTURAL CONTEXT IN TREATMENT

Most disorders have a biological base, but psychiatric illness occupies an anomalous position. As the presentation of psychiatric symptoms are the product of social, cultural, environmental, and biological variables, culture has an etiological, or modifying, role in the manifestation of mental illnesses. Therefore, family involvement as well as understanding of culture, norms, values, and expectations are important. Family-centered care is more important than individual-centered care in treating ethnic minority patients.

Expectation, rules, and agreement: It is important to note the cultural as well as the patient's expectations of what a therapist's role is, and what the therapist can do. Without understanding these rules, therapy can end with disastrous results. For example, the modern American culture expects that patients come regularly and keep their preset appointments. In Indian cultures, there is no firm rule about adhering to the time of an appointment and/or even to attending appointments. Therefore, it is not uncommon for the patient to come late or miss appointments. The therapist should not interpret this behavior as resistance or show hostile response towards the patient because of it.

Language: Language is deeply rooted in the culture of origin. Each language has its own rules, expressions, and meanings. For example, in India, no one says "I own a house or I have money." Instead the same is expressed as "Near me I have a house of money"; "I am angry" is expressed as "Anger is coming to me." For an Inuit, snow has different meanings depending on its use, whereas in English, snow is snow. In Japan, a number of words are developed to describe human relationships. An Asian girl may say "I like you" to mean that "I love you." "My house is far away" means that you are not welcome to my home. Therefore, decoding the cultural meaning of verbal communication is essential.

Nonverbal communication also needs to be interpreted carefully. In India, bride and bridegroom sit with an immobile face, not to indicate that they are unhappy, but to show the culturally adored behavior of modesty and not being moved by emotion. A patient may appear like Buddha exhibiting the culturally desirable respect for the professional. This can be mistaken for negative symptoms or disinterest. To be dependent on the physician is normal in Asian culture, as the culture makes the person interdependent from the day he is born and to keep up close family ties.

Confidentiality: Confidentiality is a legal term only pertinent in a cultural context. It is pertinent in an individually-oriented society. The same does not apply to the societies where interdependence is highly valued, where boundaries between an individual and the members of the family are fused. A physician who does not like to share an adolescent's behavior with the parents is cutting the parental authority and also offending cultural values. Confidentiality is an artificial barrier in certain cultures.

We had a patient with a huge family. The family members all wanted to come and discuss the patient. We decided that the discussion between us was completely confidential. The patient missed appointments, and when I called him, he told me that it is his family who stands up for him and guides him all the time. He told me that if I wanted to bring a wedge between him and the family, he did not need me. Afterwards, we asked the whole family to come according to the wishes of the patient. About eighteen members came, and I had to see them in a lecture room. They were eager to know the problems of the patient and wanted also to know how they could help. The very fact that they were very supportive made the patient feel overwhelmed with gratitude; the patient told me at the end of the session that he needed to improve for all of them and that he would use all the resources to get well. The family felt relieved that they were not kept in the dark. The main goal of the family was to get involved in helping.

Patient-therapist relationship: In the Western Hemisphere, psychotherapy represents an exclusive relationship where the patient comes and talks about his problems, develops insight, and thus, improves. In Asian culture, the psychotherapist is a guru who directs and mentors to bring the patient back to health. Sitting back and allowing the patient to narrate his story over and over again is not useful. The patient feels that the physician is useless and does not know how to help.

Understand the contextual meaning within the cultural context: A fifty-four-year-old woman, Subbamma, never worked, was not well educated, and had three boys of high school age. She suddenly started acting "funny" believing that she was possessed by God. She prayed for hours and would tell the fortunes of people around her. Her prestige in the neighborhood increased, but she neglected to care for her children. One day, neighbors complained to the police that she was singing loudly continuously. When she was taken to the hospital, her children and her husband came immediately to the hospital and told the physician that there was nothing wrong and that she was lucky to be possessed by God. The patient was not considered to be mentally ill. On the unit, she was not found to be psychotic, and no medications were given. She insisted on spending some time on the unit praying, which was allowed.

Upon inquiry, it was noted that her husband did not treat her well, as she was not educated and did not contribute to the family income. The children did not treat her well, either. Feeling useless and frustrated by the treatment she was receiving at home, she felt anger but could not express it. Being possessed by God gave her power and prestige. Her children were amenable to understanding that they did not treat their mother well and were willing to change. Her husband, who came from a male-dominant society, could not understand that there was anything wrong with her. However, he was willing to listen to his wife when God possessed her via God's message calling on him to treat his wife well. As a result, he started treating her with kindness. In the meantime, he became religious and started accepting his reality as it was. The family was encouraged to go to the temple and lead a life caring for each other. The priest provided the same feedback. This helped the patient, and the possession gradually faded.

Medication: Most Asians expect the physician to prescribe medications, and if no medications are prescribed, they will be disappointed and feel that the physician has no ability to understand their illnesses. A prescription, or at least telling them that they would receive the prescription as soon as the diagnosis is made, is often essential for the patient to continue treatment. Otherwise, the family will be disappointed and will consult another physician. We have worked with many patients over the years who requested a prescription during their first interview. To suggest at least multivitamin tablets is often a wise move.

Family members must feel that they are useful by participating in helping the patient, so it is sometimes advisable to leave the responsibility of giving the medications to the family. However, the head of the family may decrease the medication on his own according to the degree of improvement in the patient. Asians are familiar with consuming herbal medicines, which ordinarily do not produce detectable side-effects. At the onset of the first side-effect, the patient or the head of the family may stop the medication. Therefore, two important steps are necessary when treating an Asian family: Get the cooperation of the head of the family and get him involved in the treatment. Also, educate the family about the effects and side-effects of the medications, as well as their meaning.

Wait for the patient to express conflicts and find a compromise to fit the cultural values: A Ceylonese professional complained of headaches, which didn't improve with treatment. He looked depressed, but denied he was depressed. The headaches had persisted for several months; thus, it was recommended he see a psychiatrist. He could not provide any physical or psychological reason for his headaches. After ascertaining that his physical health was normal, the physician requested that he bring his family for the next interview. His wife and one of his sons accompanied him. During the interview, when the physician asked him about other members of the family, he and his wife started crying. He said to us that his other son, a medical student, could not come to the visit. Around the time when the headaches started, this son left medical school and wanted to marry a girl who was not acceptable to the family. The parents were not involved in this arrangement. The patient had abandoned his son because the son had deviated from the family tradition and thus brought the parents shame. While being angry with his son, he did not want to lose him. The cause of the headaches then became understandable, but a culturally acceptable solution was difficult to reach.

During subsequent sessions, the concept of abandoning a son was addressed. This led to culturally acceptable problem solving. Compromise without losing face is important in Asian culture. Ultimately, the patient came to the understanding that he did not have to give up the cultural belief that the father has the power to keep the tradition. The patient realized that he could be friendly towards his son so that he could win over time or until the son could change. Such a solution was acceptable, and thus, the son was brought back to the family with a distant hope that some day he would be a part of his father's culture.

Acceptance of the patient and the values expressed by the family: A highly respected engineer developed a slowly evolving paranoid illness. Until he became agitated, his family did not seek help. Family members finally brought the patient into the emergency room and provided a detailed history. While the engineer was in the hospital, his mother brought cookies for the psychiatrist. The psychiatrist declined the gift, explaining to her that it would serve a better purpose if the cookies were given to the patient himself, so that he could share them with other patients from the unit. A few days later, the family asked if they could take the patient to the temple, and bring him back to the hospital after offering prayers to God. The team decided not to allow him to go to the temple. The next morning, the patient was taken home by the family to see another Indian physician who accepted gifts from the patient's mother and allowed the patient to go to the temple, although accompanied at all times. The patient made a satisfactory recovery.

The first physician was not sensitive to the cultural expectations expressed by the patient's family. To share food or other gift items with the physician is culturally acceptable; and not accepting gifts is considered a rejection of their values. Similarly, going to the temple and offering prayers is a must for Indians, especially when they are sick. It is important to respect the value system of patients in order to provide them with competent and acceptable care.

Family problems should not be discussed with a stranger: We saw a Korean patient who had found out about her husband's infidelity. She felt angry and depressed, but she could not express any of these feelings, as it would displease her ancestors. Not knowing what had caused her depression, her husband brought her to the hospital. The patient refused to reveal her husband's infidelity to a stranger in front of the husband. After five or six visits, a son insisted that her husband should discuss the problem openly. The husband revealed his infidelity. Over the next two months, the patient began to improve gradually. She mentioned that she was not angry with the husband anymore, as it was not her duty to punish the husband because the deceased ancestors would do it. She, however, did not know how to live with shame in the family. Finally, the two sons and the mother agreed that they should live together in a separate home and in a city where the husband was not living, with the pretext that she had to look after her children who were going to college. This would not produce further shame for the family. The father would be respected, and the patient would look after the children. With this arrangement, and with antidepressant drugs, the patient felt better, and her depression improved.

Within the Indian culture, family members are not allowed to reveal family problems, dissensions, or conflicts to a stranger even when the stranger is a physician. The family has its own internal control, and every member should be willing to work to restore the family balance.

Interdependence, not independence, is a virtue: No member of the family is independent and therefore is controlled by other members of the family. Everyone has his or her defined role within the family and society. Each sibling is expected to assume responsibility for the younger ones, including their education. Shared and multiple parenting and strong attachment bonds with grandparents, uncles, and aunts are common. It is the duty of the children to care for their elderly parents. This helps the parents to give up their power, as well as their assets, to their children when the parents become old. Adolescents are not expected to be independent, and conformity to family norms is expected. They are not expected to leave home. Marriage is a union of two families. For adjustment problems, the young wife goes to her family to tune up her behavior and obtain emotional nurturing. Rejuvenated and equipped with new coping skills, she returns to the husband's family. The family also provides a measure of control over aggression and violence within the marriage and towards children. Ethnic minorities suffer from the absence of nurturing families when they migrate to another country. Even when the family is present, the therapist often does not recognize the advantage of working with the family.

Mother-in-law and daughter-in-law relationships are intriguing. The mother-in-law has vast power, which is sometimes unbearable to the daughter-in-law. However, the daughter-in-law bears the pain and waits for her day to become a mother-in-law herself. The sisters-in-law generally provide useful strategies to contain the mother-in-law. The power changes, and the positions, are realigned according to this predetermined rule. With the position of power also being realigned, the birth of a baby boy bestows extra power to the daughter-in-law. In-laws get preoccupied about bringing up the child within the cultural mode.

CONCLUSION

For a long time, culture has been considered as a problem to be solved in cross-cultural practice. However, culture is not a problem to be solved, but instead it is a resource for social support, problem solving, health maintenance and spiritual well-being. It is also an opportunity to meet human needs. Beyond medications and psychotherapy, human existence can be understood in the form of a four-quadrant circle: body, mind, spirit, and context. In each quadrant there is a multitude of resources on which we can rely for adjustment and coping. In the context quadrant, we can rely on family, extended kin, churches, temples or other places of worship, native healers, cultural events, and other sources of social supports. In the mind quadrant, we can rely on cultural teaching, literature, stories, metaphor, dreams, or culturally defined cognitive processes. In the body quadrant, we can rely on means of comfort, food, herbal remedies, and purification rituals such as fasting, sleep, or even dance to help patients achieve a good physiological balance. From the spiritual quadrant, we may rely on religious tools. Patients will address religious topics when they are ready to address them during treatment. Even relatives who are willing to help may sometimes address religious issues that are needed to put the patient's mind to rest for not revealing such issues previously. In summary, the patient needs to be integrated into the community and the culture.

CHAPTER TEN

DISPARITIES

Domitilo has always enjoyed a good dinner. Also, a good lunch, a good breakfast, and any good food at any time of the day or night. "I just like to eat," he says. His father died years ago at the age of forty-five, when he was already suffering complications from diabetes. The mother, not necessarily concerned about her own obesity, saw her husband's demise as the will of God. It seemed that the whole family had been destined to eat much and die young. She nonetheless was concerned that Domitilo, at age twenty-eight, couldn't be weighed on a regular scale because he already exceeded 400 pounds. Domitilo was nonplussed about our ideas regarding dieting, exercising, and even possible surgery: "We're this way . . . I am not going to change easily. It runs in the family."

Attalla had a completely different problem. She had finished training as a social worker. Full of enthusiasm and new ideas, she was accepted for an internship at a primary-care clinic. Her tuberculin test was positive, and her chest X ray showed lesions suggestive of an old inflammatory process. This alerted her and others to test the whole family. Most were equally positive. A brother and two uncles had died while still in Latin America from respiratory diseases.

In the same neighborhood, *Mrs. Buendia* was trying to recover from the sudden death of her twenty-one-year-old son, the oldest in the family. On a rainy night, young Buendia, who was competing with other auto racers, breaking all speed limits in the downtown streets at midnight, lost control of his car and died in the crash.

Lorenzo had always been good at the backbreaking work required in California's vegetable harvest. Living in his native Michoacan, Mexico, part of the year, he spent many weeks seeking a meager payment for work that often extended into the night. Lorenzo never complained, nor did he think he had a right to do so. As a child, playing Tarzan and jumping from tree to tree with other boys, he had fallen and badly damaged his left hand. With no medical help available, the hand had progressively turned into a claw that Lorenzo used mostly as a digging tool. Lorenzo was as efficient, or more so, than any other worker but was afraid that his hand would deprive him of a job. Not only did he conceal the hand quite well, he seldom spoke more than absolutely necessary.

The Chan sisters were the most popular girls in their primary school. In those days, learning that these Chinese identical twins were fully fluent in Spanish and English was astonishing to those who did not know the long history of Chinese Americans in Baja, California. This history goes back to the times when Chinese workers who had connected America by train refused to go back to China, and opted for a different life in Baja, California. The Chan girls were born in San Diego, after their mother had crossed the border looking for help with a complicated delivery. The twins were American citizens living in Tijuana and studying in San Diego. Laura completed high school, married her longtime boyfriend, and became a homemaker. Flor went on to college, became a psychologist, and joined a group of psychiatrists treating Latino and Asian patients at a minority clinic. We met them when Laura already had grandchildren, was a seemingly happy member of several minority communities, and was wrestling with obesity, high blood pressure, high cholesterol, and high blood sugar. Flor had stayed trim, was diligent about exercise and diet control, and seemed to have no medical problems to worry about.

Domitilo and his family had not associated obesity with diabetes. Neither had they thought of a relationship between their eating habits and their weight. Domitilo told us he ate well and with pleasure, but not more than other people. He really didn't know how much or how little other people ate. He was skeptical about whether his father could have lived longer if he had taken better care of himself. "God knows what He does," he said with remarkable resignation.

The thought that Attalla might have had tuberculosis as a child, that her relatives may have died from the disease, and that she may still be infected hit Attalla very hard. She reacted constructively, helped others in the family decide about treatment, and accepted a plan of treatment and follow-up. She also became a health activist.

Mrs. Buendia agreed to come to group meetings at our clinic. She soon learned that we believe many "accidents" are almost planned occurrences, often leading to destruction and death. Her son had undertaken a high-risk game, and he had lost. He was not the first, and certainly not the last, in his generation who would risk his life while thinking of himself as invincible.

Lorenzo's fall during his childhood had maimed him for life; it had affected his emotional health and his perceived ability to work. It had also modified his social life and his ambitions. Though his courage and determination had helped a great deal, he had suffered throughout his life. He didn't think that medical intervention might have led to a very different situation.

The health of ethnic minorities in the United States is not as good as the health of others. This statement is accepted by most in the big national debate about disparities in health. The questions are abundant: What is the role of genetics? What about poverty? Would everyone fare the same if offered the same services? If the situation is going to change, who will be the most effective agent of change? The government? Ethnic minorities themselves as a group? Each individual? Is change possible?

Domitilo's family may follow our advice and start preventive measures among the children in future generations, but who will convince Domitilo that he has to lose weight? Attalla did not have adequate care as a child; she now is a patient advocate. Do we need or want many Attallas? What about the Buendias? Who should participate in preventing car crashes resulting from reckless behavior? What are the lessons to be learned about Lorenzo's handicap? The Chan girls were identical as children; as they advanced in age, they were medically different; genetic factors seem to count earlier in life while environmental factors seem to be more important late in life. How do these issues apply to ethnic minorities?

UNEQUAL TREATMENT

The Institute of Medicine (IOM) Report, "Unequal Treatment: Confronting Racial and Ethnic Disparities in Healthcare," concluded that "[al]though a myriad of sources contribute to these disparities, some evidence suggests that bias, prejudice, and stereotyping on the part of healthcare providers may contribute to differences in care." (Note 10–1).

Most studies find disparities in clinical services that are equally effective for all racial and ethnic groups. Studies reviewed by the IOM suggest that racial differences in patients' attitudes, such as their preferences for treatment, do not vary greatly and do not fully explain racial and ethnic disparities in health care. IOM tried to answer a key question: If minority patients' attitudes toward health care and preferences for treatment are not likely to be a major source of healthcare disparities, what other factors may contribute to these disparities? IOM considered two sets of factors.

The first set of factors include those related to the operation of healthcare systems and the legal and regulatory climate in which they operate. These include cultural and linguistic barriers, fragmentation of healthcare systems (ethnic minorities may be disproportionately enrolled in lower-cost health plans that place greater per-patient lim-

its on health care expenditures and available services), and where
ethnic minorities tend to receive care (for example, ethnic minorities
are less likely to access care in a private physician's office, even when
insured at the same level as others). The second set of factors refers
to the actual clinical encounter. Three mechanisms that lead to disparities in care may be in operation:

1. ***Bias (or prejudice) against ethnic minorities***: Prejudice
   is defined as an unjustified negative attitude based on a
   persons' group membership. The IOM report states,
   "Survey research suggests that among white Americans
   prejudicial attitudes towards ethnic minorities remain more
   common than not, as over half to three-quarters believe
   that relative to whites, ethnic minorities—particularly
   African Americans—are less intelligent, more prone to violence, and prefer to live off welfare. It is reasonable to
   assume, however, that the vast majority of healthcare
   providers find prejudice morally abhorrent and at odds with
   their professional values. But healthcare providers, like
   other members of society, may not recognize manifestations
   of prejudice in their own behavior." The IOM report cites a
   study based on actual clinical encounters. It found that doctors rated black patients as less intelligent, less educated,
   more likely to abuse drugs and alcohol, more likely to fail to
   comply with medical advice, more likely to lack social support, and less likely to participate in cardiac rehabilitation
   than white patients, even after patients' income, education,
   and personality characteristics were taken into account.
2. ***Medical decisions under time pressure with limited
   information***: Physicians are often trained to rely on clusters of information that function as prototypes or stereo-
   typic constellations. When there is incomplete or inaccurate
   information, which occurs more frequently when medical
   decisions are made under time pressure, there is an
   ever-present danger that prejudices may be major factors

influencing the physician's attitudes, strategies, and final decisions.

3. ***Patient response: mistrust and refusal*:** Ethnic minority patients may come to the clinical encounter with a history of negative racial experiences in other contexts, or be subjected to real or perceived mistreatment by professionals. If patients convey mistrust, refuse treatment, or comply poorly with treatment, professionals may be less engaged in the treatment process, and patients may not get effective treatments or services. Patients and professionals may influence each other, and their interaction may reflect the attitudes, expectations, and perceptions that each may have developed in situations where race and ethnicity are more prominent than the participants realize.

4. ***Cross-cultural education*:** Stereotypes, bias, and clinical uncertainty may influence diagnostic and treatment decisions, as pointed out above. Cross-cultural education may enhance health professionals' information on how cultural and social factors influence health care, thus adding strategies to obtain, negotiate, and manage this information clinically. Cross-cultural education refers to *attitudes* (cultural sensitivity/awareness approach), *knowledge* (multicultural/ categorical approach), and *skills* (cross-cultural approach). Experience so far has been positive in using this approach to improve knowledge of cultural and behavioral aspects of health care and to build effective communication strategies.

Unequal treatment advocates for the collection of standardized data. The hope is that data on the race and ethnicity of patient and provider will allow researchers to better understand factors associated with healthcare disparities, ensure accountability, improve patient choices, allow for the evaluation of methods of intervention, and help identify discriminatory practices. Data collection, in our opinion, can be effective only when conducted in full cooperation with the groups affected.

THE AMA'S COUNCIL ON SCIENTIFIC AFFAIRS' REPORT ON RACIAL AND ETHNIC DISPARITIES IN HEALTH CARE

Minority race or ethnicity has been linked to a lesser chance of having a regular source of care, fewer physician visits, less-intensive hospital visits, and total healthcare expenditures. Minority race and ethnicity are risk factors for less care along a wide range of services. Minority race or ethnicity has been linked to disparities in cancer diagnostic tests and treatment; screening, diagnostic, and therapeutic interventions for heart disease and stroke; diabetes care; clinical procedures for cerebrovascular disease; HIV care; renal transplantation; asthma care; and other preventive and specialty health services. (Note 10–2).

LINKING DISPARITIES AND HEALTHCARE OUTCOMES

"While the connection appears intuitive, disparities in health care have only recently been linked directly to disparities in health care outcomes. In part, this is because health care outcomes may be a consequence of a number of factors of which health care is only one. These include but are not limited to: socioeconomic status, genetics, risk behavior, disaffiliation, geographic location, residential segregation, and discrimination. While population studies suggest that medical care makes only a limited contribution to health status outcomes, the relative impact of health care is much greater for racial and ethnic minorities due to the existence of multiple vulnerabilities."

WHY HEALTH DISPARITIES EXIST

The factors presented here by the AMA Council on Scientific Affairs match those discussed by the Institute of Medicine. Health insurance coverage and income combined typically account for less than half of the disparities observed. Studies of ethnic minority patients suggest that they may delay treatment or adhere poorly to treatment regimens. These behaviors may be related to lack of familiarity with disease/treatment, mistrust of physicians or the health care system, poor prior interactions with the health care system, or poor recall of, or a misunderstanding of, instructions.

The relative influence of the patient, the system and the professional in creating disparities is complex and poorly understood. Patient factors may actually account for the least amount of variation in health utilization; thus, suggesting that greater responsibility for racial and ethnic disparities in health care, independent of access, may fall on the system or the provider. The organization of the health care system may be the most influential; the professional's uncertainty, bias and beliefs may be enhanced by time pressures and resource restrictions that eliminate patient-centered care.

PROFESSIONALISM

Significant differences exist between the business community and health professionals. A critical difference is the interest of physicians in human conditions affecting large communities. We want to use the tools of population-based medicine (PBM) to improve health care for racial and ethnic minorities. By placing the individual within the context of a large community of both sick and healthy individuals, PBM attempts to manage the health care of a population as a whole.

ADDRESSING DISPARITIES

Building a case for addressing disparities is an effort at determining the relevance of many factors.

Will genetic research address health disparities? The answer is that genetic considerations will be helpful in evaluating factors that affect drug metabolism and hereditary disorders, but may not directly contribute to addressing racial or cultural disparities.

In the 2003 *New England Journal of Medicine* article "Race and Genomics," the authors explain, "Health disparities and genetics may have little to do with each other, short of both capturing public attention simultaneously. The irony is that if we do not recognize that they are distinct, if interrelated, topics, efforts that are meant to improve the health of racial and ethnic minorities instead might inadvertently harm them, which could happen if genetic research diverts attention from productive ideas about the effects of environment on health or if it reinforces racial and ethnic stereotypes that contribute to the very discrimination that health disparities initiatives are meant to ameliorate." (Note 10–3).

Short of selective problems or advantages resulting from genetic factors that influence drug metabolism, genetic factors related to a small group of hereditary illnesses, and genetic factors that may possibly influence behaviors (i.e., drinking habits), genetics may not be a productive area of help in eliminating disparities.

A List of Disparity Factors

Genetics: Not likely to be productive, as mentioned above.

Housing: Most members of ethnic minority groups live in substandard housing. They live in places made hazardous by lead-paint-coated walls and defective, fire-prone heating systems. They are exposed to allergens produced "by cockroach and rat infestations and the indoor pesticides used to control them." (Note 10–3). Neighborhoods where housing is available to ethnic minorities are often below ambient air quality standards and often located near hazardous sites.

Jobs: Many members of ethnic minority groups accept health risks through exposure to toxic chemicals used in manufacturing or agriculture. Their jobs require long periods of backbreaking activity, excessive physical labor, repetitive strain on key joints, lack of breaks in monotony, lack of positive incentives, and minimal personal respect and opportunities for promotion. We have no doubt that minority members have had good positions in many areas of endeavor. The fact is that there are not enough ethnic minorities in key positions, many have no chance to get there, and the decision-makers are not necessarily in favor of advancing ethnic minorities.

Emotional stress: Many members of ethnic minority groups are subjected to harassment, discrimination, and minimal respect for their rights. Several of our patients were victims of intimidation when they were about to vote in the 2004 presidential election. One of them spent the small amount of time he had expected to spend away from work in order to vote in detention. Though American born and carrying full identification, this patient had to wait several hours before he was allowed to leave. The officer who kept him from voting said our patient "should be happy no charges were filed against him."

Inadequate health insurance: Ethnic minority members are excessively represented among the uninsured, even though more than 80 percent work regularly at steady jobs. We believe that adequate healthcare coverage will happen only when most people decide to take care of their own health. Ethnic minorities should be among the people most interested in health coverage that doesn't include the government or employers.

Poverty: We chose to mention poverty on its own, because very often those addressing disparities fail to mention that lack of money interferes with the emotional health of ethnic minorities. That mental health and social class are inversely related has been known for many years. (Note 10–4). The classic study by Hollingshead and Redlich was followed by a ten-year follow-up of clinic and inpatient hospital patients that demonstrated the somber prognosis of the poorest patients. Their disorders were more severe and resulted in serious unemployment, financial problems, and a high degree of social isolation. If treated in hospitals, these patients faced the prospect of returning to a community without friends, sufficient income, or adequate housing. On top of all these obstacles, they faced the stigma attached to mental illness, which would make it more difficult for them to be employed. The findings obtained in research conducted many decades ago regarding poverty and mental illnesses are still relevant today.

California board-and-care homes were created in the 1960s in response to "de-institutionalization." They were intended to insure a level of care in the community equal to or better than the care provided by state hospitals in the past. What is the reality today? Continuity of care is fragmented or nonexistent. Quality of services is in most cases, poor or worse. The number of unlicensed homes is rising. Against the intention of the creators of these facilities, for many psychiatric patients unlicensed homes have become permanent housing. Given the budgets and the patients' needs, many live in squalor with no hope of progress. When the San Diego Coalition of Mental Health surveyed 201 residents in 1998, most complained about lack of medical care, most said they were not included in making house rules, and 46 percent reported violence in their homes.

Even in the absence of emotional difficulties, lack of money means many problems, including the following:

Lack of awareness of health and illness: The individual may spend a lot of time trying to survive from day to day, so that ideas about exercise, nutrition, sleep, early manifestations of illness, or just strategies to stay and feel well may be absent.

Lack of social contacts: Home-and-board-care residents are mostly the newcomers to a community, but many others have difficulty making contacts with neighbors, co-workers, and even members of the same ethnic minority group. The resulting alienation and isolation are hindrances to adaptation.

Lack of opportunities: Because of lack of social interaction, there is minimal awareness of the usual occupational or social ladders that lead to a better life. Even when some awareness of such ladders exists, the individual may believe he is not a candidate to use them.

Lack of awareness of illness: In the midst of multiple stresses and minimal outside help, the individual may not pay attention to symptoms that will further handicap him.

Lack of awareness of rights: Lack of communication may prevent the person from learning about benefits he has paid for, free programs that may benefit him, or even places where he can go for information and help at no charge.

Family disruption: The breadwinner who works for minimal wages often lacks the time or the tools to become a good family leader. Children growing up in squalid conditions are not likely to identify with their parents. For many, belonging to a gang and wearing its colors and tattoos may seem the easiest opportunity towards a role in society.

Mortality: Although many conditions contribute to socioeconomic and racial disparities and in potential life-years lost, a few conditions account for most of these disparities. That is the case with smoking-related diseases vis-à-vis mortality among persons with fewer years of education, hypertension, HIV, diabetes mellitus, and trauma among black persons. In the 2003 *New England Journal of Medicine* article "Contribution of Major Disease to Disparities in Mortality," the authors Cooper, Kaufman, and Ward write, "Given limited resources to eliminate health disparities, we need to focus our efforts in order to achieve the maximum gains. Our data suggest that targeting ischemic heart disease and lung cancer would be the most useful in reducing the overall disparities in mortality; whereas targeting hypertension, HIV, trauma, and diabetes would have the greatest effect on the racial disparity." (Note 10–5).

Quality improvement strategies affecting diabetes and its complications should help in decreasing treatment outcome disparities and reducing mortality among ethnic minorities. The Centers for Medicare and Medicaid Services funded a quality improvement project involving monitoring of patient outcomes, feedback of performance data, and education of clinicians at dialysis centers between 1993 and 2000.

In 1993, 46 percent of white patients and 36 percent of black patients received an adequate hemodialyisis dose compared with 2000 when the proportions were 87 percent and 84 percent respectively, so that the gap between white and black patients decreased from 10 percent to 3 percent. (Note 10–6). Similarly, we hope to see more positive findings in many quality improvement projects.

THE RESULTS OF DISPARITIES

In their 2003 *New England Journal of Medicine* article "Race and Genomics," authors Cooper, Kaufman, and Ward present stark evidence of the results of healthcare disparities:

"Shorter lives are the price that Black, Hispanic, and American Indian and Alaskan Native populations pay for inadequate health care, unsafe living conditions, and high psychological stress. The average life expectancy of White men is 74 years and of Black men, 66 years. Although this figure represents a gain for Black men of several years since 1960, it is still lower than that reported for Whites more than 40 years ago. Among American Indian males, the average life expectancy remains in the mid-50s, exactly where it was in 1960. These inequalities are mirrored in childhood mortality data. Despite notable improvements in neonatal outcomes, children younger than one year born to Black mothers have a greater mortality rate than infants born to White or Asian mothers, and neonates born at very low birth weights (lower than 1500 g) are 3 times more likely to have Black than White mothers." (Note 10–7).

ARE THERE SUFFICIENT DOCTORS TO HELP MINORITIES?

In October of 2003, the United States General Accounting Office issued a Physician Workforce report entitled "Physician Supply Increased in Metropolitan and Nonmetropolitan Areas, but Geographic Disparities Persisted." The report stated:

> "The U.S. physician population increased 26 percent, which was twice the rate of the total population growth, between 1991 and 2001. During this period, the average number of physicians per 100,000 people increased from 214 to 239, and the mix of generalists and specialists in the national physician workforce remained about one-third generalists and two-thirds specialists. The growth in physician supply per 100,000 people between 1991 and 2001 was seen in historically high-supply metropolitan areas as well as low-supply statewide nonmetropolitan areas." (Note 10–8).

From the viewpoint of ethnic minorities, studies like this may not contribute much to our understanding of actual disparities in care. Those who deal with ethnic minorities know that we do not have enough physicians to see them. Global figures tend to be misleading. The Health Resources and Services Administration has commented on the General Accounting Office report as follows:

> "We note with concern that despite some progress, rural citizens still are served by roughly half as many physicians per 100,000 as the total United States population, with only 12 percent of the decade's physician population increase going to nonmetropolitan areas. The healthcare workforce in rural areas and related issues that contribute to the problem clearly need con-

tinued support and attention. We will continue to support efforts to address the geographic disparities your report conveys to the best of our abilities.

"The history of the Health Professional Shortage Area and Medically Underserved Area designations has shown that many people lack access even in an area with a large number of physicians. This lack of access is often due to economic facts. Lack of insurance, Medicaid coverage, or low income in general may prevent many residents from receiving care from many of the physicians in the area. In addition, there may be language and cultural barriers that keep the residents from seeking or receiving appropriate care. While geographic distribution is a useful, higher level way to assess supply, it does not tell the entire story.

". . . The study does not provide additional substance to a discussion of the adequacy of that supply or distribution with respect to the health care needs of the U.S. population. The study does not mention disease burden or health insurance coverage rates in those geographic areas studied. The report does mention some of the health care infrastructure factors which affect physician practice, such as access to specialists, but lacks a discussion on the degree to which infrastructure factors such as hospital access are involved." (Note 10–9).

Our experience justifies the concerns expressed by the Health Resources and Services Administration: underserved areas, often with large minority populations, are frequently in the same regional area where other, wealthier populations, enjoy some of the best medical services in the country.

We believe that there is a shortage of physicians in the U.S., and it will get worse. Using a planning model that couples economic growth to healthcare spending and physician demand, Dr. Richard A. Cooper, from the Medical College of Wisconsin in Milwaukee, has estimated that by 2020, there could be a shortage of 200,000 doctors, or about 20 percent of the required workforce. (Note 10–10).

OUR OWN PHYSICIANS

Ethnic minorities are woefully under-represented in U.S. medical schools. The percentage of Black and Latino medical students is far below their representation in the general population, which has created a deficit in medical care. Many of the health disparities happen among ethnic minorities who live in underserved areas.

Remedial action, often discussed among those interested in correcting disparities, includes recruiting potential medical students at all levels, starting in high school and in college; mentoring students as they advance into medical school; creating a supportive atmosphere in medical school; and familiarizing medical students, interns, and residents with the plight of ethnic minorities and the challenges in serving them. We appreciate that the medical care of ethnic minorities will continue to be given mostly by non-minority physicians. Ideally, they and all physicians will acquire the cultural competence required to advance beyond current disparities in care. In the meantime, ethnic minorities have to endeavor to train their own physicians, and this has to be a major goal for each ethnic minority group.

Currently, many ethnic minority groups benefit from the presence of international medical graduates. These physicians have received their medical education in medical schools in other countries, have passed the necessary examinations, and have obtained residency training and licenses in the United States. They are highly over-represented in underserved areas. As long as there are insufficient numbers of ethnic minority physicians trained in the U.S., the international medical graduates will continue to be critical to the care of ethnic minority patients in rural areas and in the poor neighborhoods of the cities. Even with their contribution, according to the General Accounting Report mentioned above, seventeen metropolitan areas, including Los Angeles–Long Beach, experienced declines in the number of physicians per 100 people in the ten-year period covered by the report.

FINANCING HEALTH CARE FOR MINORITIES

Ethnic minorities have done very poorly in the current U.S. health financing "nonsystem." They are excessively represented among the working poor who will never get health insurance from employers or from government programs. Attempts at changing this situation should consider the following:

Federal tax exemptions and other tax benefits should be awarded to individual employees and not to employers or to any other intermediaries. Federal tax adjustments could go a long way towards financing health coverage for all Americans. Starting with those barely above the poverty level, tax vouchers could be given to people living in poverty, so that they could have access to health financing. Additionally, catastrophic insurance should be available to all Americans. The deductible amount would be high enough that everyone would be covered primarily for expenses that go beyond those an individual can budget for health care. Full-coverage insurance should be avoided. Research has shown that health expenses increase when the individual has no responsibility for costs.

Research also shows that both prevention of illness and effective treatment depend on habits. We propose that the medical community share with ethnic minorities all we know about prevention through reasonable health protection, so that the individual becomes the master of his/her own health. Best practices may be expensive, and the individual needs to be prepared to always think about a health budget. The individual and his/her family are the direct beneficiaries of enhanced well-being and more productive, longer lives and, thus, should be prepared to pay their share of the costs.

HOW ARE WE DOING?

Ed Koch, the former Mayor of New York, would stop people on the street to ask, "How am *I* doing?" We have done the same among ourselves. *I* has become *we*. Writing this book made us more aware of where the ethnic minorities in the United States have been, and where we would like them to be. We are coming from years of misunderstanding, confrontation, struggles and occasional discouragements, to a period when we can see the beginning of substantial achievements: minorities will join others as equal partners in seeking the fulfillment of the American dream.

As is usually the case, we are standing on the shoulders of giants. Many years after the beginning of key initiatives, those in the past who believed in minorities, devoted their lives to improving the lot of their minority peers, and mapped the territories we want to explore guide us today. Most of them were known but by a few in their communities. We want to recognize some who stand for all the unsung advocates who have blazed the trail toward better health for the minorities.

David

David E. Hayes-Bautista, researcher, scientist, and man of the people, keeps on thinking of minorities. Which ones? Probably every one from every origin who feels like Texans do.

David explains:

A senior reporter from a large east coast newspaper decided to write about Latinos. He interviewed David and asked the question that every outsider asks: "Are you primarily a Latino, or primarily an American?" In the process of answering, David created the best definition of minorities we have seen: "When you ask me that question, you are implying that Latino is not American, or that maybe it's un-American. It's not being anti-American; it's like being a Texan, it's a *distinctive* way of being American."

There was plenty of irony in Dr. Hayes-Bautista's analogy. As a historian and sociologist, he knew that much of the Texan identity derived from a clash of cultures: the British colonists were farmers on foot. The Spaniards were men on horseback who drove herds of cattle from one open range to another. As the Spanish way of herding cattle became established in Texas, many Spanish words became new Texan words, including the quintessential one: Cowboy, a new way of pronouncing and spelling an old Spanish word. (Note 11–1).

Laura

She could be a doting grandmother, a wonderful and giving family member, the ideal neighbor and the listening partner of all those in pain. She was also as hard as the hardest warrior. Laura's desire to provide health services to the *Barrio* led her and her followers to take control of a dilapidated county building, uninhabited, in the early 1970s. The police came. The sergeant in charge, himself a Latino, chose negotiation rather than confrontation, and eventually an agreement emerged that left Laura in physical possession of the house she wanted. It has been a construction site ever since. The modest initial building has been transformed into an ever-enlarging architectural wonder.

The first professionals at the clinic were all volunteers, mostly nurses, social workers, teachers, retired physicians, and physicians willing to donate a few hours at a time. From the beginning, in a poor neighborhood afflicted by all the ills of poverty and exposure to vandals and transients, the clinic remained startlingly white, with no graffiti, and no damage marks.

Many years later, the clinic has become a growing medical complex with services and interactions that permit full medical care, mostly at the clinic, but also linked to the best hospitals in town, usually provided by key physicians who donate their services.

We started almost from the beginning of the clinic to advocate for psychiatric services. Even when we had positions of leadership, we could not advance our ideas because of a myriad of pressing medical problems that drained time and funds. Many years later, the obstacles were overcome, and the first psychiatric center at the clinic was started. It had a shaky beginning that gave way to strong growth and diversification of services.

Today, the clinic started by Laura in the Barrio provides services in twelve sites around the County of San Diego. Six of them already have psychiatric programs. These programs are the fastest growing among all the initiatives under our new umbrella, Family Health Centers.

From the beginning, the clinic has been owned by the Latino community, and takes pride in noting that 70 percent of the support comes from payments made by patients, many of whom have minimal incomes. The remaining money comes from grants for specific services or research, and grants from a diversity of foundations.

Laura has been dead for a number of years, but lives in our hearts and in the medical services our community enjoys.

EXCELLENCE AMONG THE POOR

When Dr. Richard Butcher graduated at the top of his class and had the opportunity to study medicine any place in the country, he chose Meharry Medical College. "I wanted to have a clear understanding of my people and their needs. A traditional minority school was more likely to provide the tools I needed in my practice." If one listens to his patients, he was right. His tendency to make room for anyone who needed or wanted to see him, soon converted his waiting room into a smaller version of Grand Central Station. His insistence that everyone had to be seen led him to work increasingly longer hours. This did not prevent him from being very active in a number of medical organizations, which eventually led to the Presidency of the National Medical Association (NMA).

Dr. Rodney Hood joined Dr. Butcher after a brilliant career at the University of California. It soon became clear that he would follow in Dr. Butcher's steps. As President of the NMA, Dr. Hood promoted a better understanding of disparities in medical care, which has made lecturing and advocating two of his major occupations.

After many years and successive expansions, the offices of Drs. Butcher and Hood have progressively specialized in the areas of medicine most relevant to minorities. They are still surrounded by the homes of those they have chosen to treat, regardless of the financial pressures produced by myopic state and federal initiatives.

The continuity of Drs. Butcher's and Hood's efforts is now assured by the presence in their offices of younger physicians who share their vision of medicine. The combination of social action and excellence in medical services that Dr. Butcher and Dr. Hood espouse is likely to become a model for all of those who want to create the parameters for the practice of medicine in states with diverse populations, which will soon be all of the states in the union.

Francis and the APA

We recently sat across the table from Francis Lu, Chair of the APA
Council on Minority Health and Mental Health Disparities, at a
meeting that discussed better training for minority psychiatrists. We
couldn't stop ourselves from reflecting about the many times we had,
over a period of several decades, listened to Dr. Lu discuss the history of minorities in the United States, the problems of minority
patients in university settings, the influence of cultural factors in the
diagnosis and treatment of psychiatric disorders, and many other
subjects related to ethnic minorities.

A clinician, researcher, teacher and administrator, Dr. Lu seems
to cover all the areas relevant to the progress of these minorities. He
has been at the forefront, and we appreciate it. We appreciate it even
more when we remember that the path towards success in helping
minorities includes many defeats, but also key victories.

In Francis, we also see those whose efforts will never be fully
recognized. Central to any recognition is Jeanne Spurlock, who was
the relentless and uncompromising leader of ethnic minorities in
the APA for a quarter of a century. She was not the first advocate,
and her efforts would not have been possible without those of the
pioneers.

Jeanne

There were two phases in the early struggles of ethnic minorities.
The first one started with the minority heroes of WWII. The exploits
of the Black battalions, of the Nisan warriors and of the Latino win-
ners of many Medals of Honor, prepared ethnic minorities to make
the efforts necessary to be recognized as truly American. This phase
created the basis for the ethnic minority movement in organized psychiatry.

The second phase began with the efforts by African-American
psychiatrists to obtain an equal footing in the structure and the

decision-making process of the APA. Those who study the ensuing process may wonder about tokenism: Several illustrious Black psychiatrists became officers of the APA, but none advanced to President. In the process, the Office of Director of Minority Affairs was created, and Jeanne Spurlock became the first Director. Our many conversations with her leave little room for speculation about her goals. She saw herself as a minority of one who was likely to be misunderstood, undervalued, and often bypassed. She wanted to create the basis for actions that might be taken long after she was dead.

Jeanne faced a future she had not predicted: she was part of an American process in which even her own family became less Black, the brown people became predominantly Latino and Asian, and newcomers became part of the equation.

Beginning in the early 1960s, the proportion of Foreign Medical Graduates, later called International Medical Graduates (IMGs)—we did not feel very foreign, but felt as American as International—began to increase, to the point that today more than 40 percent of practicing psychiatrists in the United States may belong to this group.

Jeanne had difficulty accepting IMGs as minorities and as representatives of the minorities. Nevertheless, she was willing to accept us as allies in the many struggles the ethnic minorities undertook during the last decades of the last century.

Dr. Spurlock's years in the APA were the time when ethnic minorities established their presence in the APA structure. Committees and Councils were created that assured the participation of minority psychiatrists at most levels of decision making. Those who worked in the process thought that the initial progress couldn't be stopped. We were wrong. When Jeanne left, the power that initially had seemed solid and sustainable began to decrease. The APA Office on Minority Affairs disappeared.

Today it is positioned to grow again. The office has been budgeted, and it is in excellent hands. The challenges are many and difficult, but we as ethnic minorities believe that we have the leadership, the assets, and the will to fulfill our goals.

Ruben

Late in 2004, Latinos were surprised to learn that one of us had received the McArthur Award, whish carried with it half a million dollars that Mr. Ruben Martinez could spend in any way he wanted. But, who was Mr. Martinez?

Mr. Martinez of Santa Ana, California had spent most of his adult years as a barber. He loved education, books, ideas, and debate—but not the nice debate often carried out by friendly neighbors who may want to talk about the next football game. Mr. Martinez wanted to talk about people, their suffering, their hopes, and their future. He wanted to document his arguments by referring to his favorite books, both in Spanish and in English. He kept them handy, and began to lend them to an increasing number of customers. Some people wanted to keep the books, so Mr. Martinez started selling them. His barber shop gradually became an excellent book store.

One day in the mid 1990s, Mr. Martinez, already in his 50s, stopped cutting hair and became a book store owner. The store faced unusual challenges: it was located in an ostensibly non-intellectual, depreciated, and poor neighborhood. It had to support itself with funds coming from people who didn't include books in the monthly budget. It had to look as if Mr. Martinez meant business, even if the business would kill him.

When we visited Mr. Martinez, the store occupied 3,000 square feet. It was enclosed in glass. It had wide alleys and places to sit, read, and argue. It had an art gallery. It had just expanded to a nearby building that housed the children's section and the store's auditorium. Mr. Martinez's numerous customers appeared to be old friends. All seemed to be taking books home. Most were by known Spanish writers. Ruben told us the average purchase was $50.00, usually paid in cash.

Mr. Martinez gave us the red-carpet treatment, which included a full inspection of the adult and the children's stores, a discussion of the artist displaying his art at the moment, lunch at his favorite Mexican restaurant, and full explanations of why we have to bring health issues to the attention of every Latino. Mr. Martinez was very proud to show us his health section. He even apologized about the apparently excessive representation of publications on sex, sexual life, and measures towards a happier sex life. We explained that we are in favor of anything that contributes to our people's well being.

Mr. Martinez's second book store is in Lynnwood, California, another place with financial problems. Mr. Martinez has a 5,000 square foot site there. "If I survive and attract other people, I'll repeat the Santa Ana miracle. In Santa Ana, we managed to bring along a restaurant, a beauty parlor, a hotel, a set of condos, and even a funeral home."

We happened to agree that literacy and health go together. Mr. Martinez is coming to San Diego to see if we can start his third book store close to where the barrio clinic began.

Yolanda

How do we make our communities aware of solutions to mental health problems? Yolanda has spent much of her life involved in community projects in northern Mexico. Her interests have been the arts, folklore, music, and representation of history and shared values in the daily life of a community. For the last three years, with help from the Depressive-Bipolar Disorder Support Alliance, and using the Alliance's material in Spanish, she has started a support center that represents the efforts of people who have recovered from depression and want to help others understand and seek treatment for the illness. She has learned much about the immense barriers that keep most potential patients from getting help. Her center represents an ever-expanding source of information that can be replicated elsewhere in Mexico and other countries.

Like Yolanda, we believe that our patients become much more effective in combating mental illness when their advocates manage to influence key decision makers in each community.

Linda and Nikki

One of our psychiatric clinics for Latinos happens to have an African-American coordinator. Linda, the coordinator, began her career as an advocate while studying to become a counselor. After obtaining her license, she became a constant advocate for minorities. She was not a newcomer when she agreed to work mostly with Latinos. Nikki emerged in the Latino community, speaking both English and Spanish. She was a natural for her present job. Our minority clients are constant reminders that there are many more similarities than differences among seemingly different ethnic groups.

FILTERS AND CHALLENGES

Eustaquio's brother-in-law, a rancher in the Mexican State of Tijuana, received Yolanda's help because 36 years ago he seemed to be dying from a rare disease. Within a period of three months, Eustaquio had abandoned his ranch, stayed mostly behind closed doors in his bedroom, lost more than 40 pounds, slept poorly, and spoke less and less—until, for more than two weeks, his communication was mostly via gestures.

During this time, Eustaquio had been mostly sitting on his bed, motionless and staring at the wall. A number of diagnostic studies conducted by the family physician had been negative, so that the nature and the treatment of the disorder were a mystery to the family.

Two facts directed the family to consult with Yolanda: Eustaquio's mother had committed suicide in her thirties and Eustaquio's brother had inspected his bedroom, and found a large collection of knives.

Yolanda proposed that studies be done to rule out a psychotic depression. This is how Eustaquio became our patient. When we first saw him, Eustaquio looked catatonic; he wouldn't talk and he kept staring in front of him.

In a period of two weeks, Eustaquio responded well to a substantial amount of medication.

One month later, he impressed the clinic staff when he came back displaying his ranch regalia, including the characteristic hat, belt, and boots. He looked and acted as if he was full of vim and vigor. We communicated to the family our fear that he might, now, go into a manic episode. They said that Eustaquio's very expansive stance and demeanor were typical for him. We still insisted in continuing the medication and planning a long term follow-up.

In reviewing with Eustaquio his feelings and thoughts at the peak of his disease, we learned that he had felt paralyzed by fear; he had heard voices telling him to kill himself; and, eventually, he'd come to the conclusion that he was doomed to die soon.

He now realizes all of this was alien to him and to his life.

We knew Eustaquio's mother had not received psychiatric care, and her death had been a surprise to the family. Eustaquio's behavior had also been surprising, and had been attributed to a physical illness. The link to our clinic was not the physicians seeing her, but the family's recollection that Yolanda had gone around talking about the many manifestations of depression and its relationship to suicide.

The current neglect of the diagnosis and treatment of depression in minority communities may not become less harmful until many community advocates create the bridge between the patient and the mental health community. We would like the primary physician to be more of a link, and hope to see several factors change:

1. Family physicians, internists, gynecologists and pediatricians should be trained to at least include psychiatric disorder in every differential diagnosis. This is not happening today.

2. Physicians who have the first opportunity to evaluate a patient should give due attention to psychiatric disorders. During the first interview with a new patient, there should be an opportunity to explore or dismiss psychiatric disorders. At the very least, the patient should be able to complete a screening questionnaire on the

most common disorders. Our experience to date, when leaving such a questionnaire at our colleagues' offices, has been disappointing.

3. Physicians are penalized for using psychiatric diagnoses. If Medicare covers the patient and the patient has a depression accompanied by headaches, the doctor is paid twice as much if the diagnosis is headache and not depression.

4. Physicians in primary care are paid for volume. A difficult differential diagnosis leading to a psychiatric disorder may be emotionally and intellectually rewarding, but may require time that insurance companies and others will not allow.

5. Even if the family physician makes a psychiatric diagnosis and wants to refer a patient to a psychiatrist, she may find that the few remaining psychiatrists in the community are very taxed by their other patients as most communities today have fewer psychiatrists than they need.

6. Psychiatrists have not been deeply involved in programs promoting close interaction among all the professionals who examine and treat patients with psychiatric disorders. The American Psychiatric Association and The Academy of Family Practice are engaged in several pilot studies that may progressively increase communications and professional interaction.

7. Large and ambitious research programs should involve key professional associations. (Note 11–2).

Jacky Sans

Jacky has dark skin, black eyes, black hair, and is not very tall. He told us in confidence that, as far as he knew, his real name was Jacinto Santos. He knew he had been born in Salinas, California. He learned this by accident:

He was at the Metropolitan Correctional Institute in San Diego, about to be deported to Mexico, when a social worker found that a

Jacinto Santos, with the same date of birth and recorded parents as Jacky Sans, had been born in Salinas. He had grown up in a succession of foster homes; his foster parents had changed his name and he had never spoken Spanish.

Jacky had come to San Diego to discover that growing communities were ready for new newspaper routes. After delivering the daily paper to a large number of customers in the same community for several months, he started hiring others to do the same. He then thought that he could help them to buy economy cars to become more efficient. Fred, the rich man in the neighborhood, offered to help—if he got 50 percent of the business. Very soon, Fred was supplying Jacky's carriers with older cars they could use. After a number of months of prosperity, and precisely when Jacky wanted to expand the business to other cities in Southern California, he found himself arrested for a number of federal felonies, not the least of which was buying and selling stolen cars. Considered an illegal immigrant, he ended up in the federal penitentiary, the Metropolitan Correctional Institute, awaiting extradition to Mexico, a country he had never visited. After a number of lucky events and much legal help, Jacky found himself free, with no legal record, and an American citizen for the first time in his life.

Jacky may never know it, but he is a member of the large group of Californians that will define the future of the State. Here are the facts. (Note 11–3):

From 3.6 million in 1980, California's foreign-born population grew to 9.8 million in 2005, and at the current level of immigration, is projected to grow further to 14.1 million by 2030. The share of the population comprised of the foreign born surged from 15.1 percent in 1980 to 27 percent in 2005 and is projected to rise much more slowly, reaching 29.8 percent in 2030.

The second generation (the children of the immigrant first generation) is beginning to grow rapidly. Among children ages 5 to 14, only 9.6 percent are foreign born today, while a full 36 percent are second generation, more than double the 14.8 percent in 1980. Less than 10 percent of school age children are immigrants: 54.4 percent are third generation, 36 percent are second generation, and only 9.6 percent are foreign born. Among adults ages 25 to 34, Jacky's cohort, only 5.6 percent were second generation in 1980, rising to 13.1 percent in 2005, and anticipated to reach 26.7 percent in 2030.

The average length of residence in the U.S. of immigrants is rapidly rising. Among Latinos, the average length of U.S. residence of the foreign-born rose from 12.1 years in 1980 to 14.6 in 2005 and is anticipated to rise to 22.5 years in 2030. Among Asians, the comparable figures are 10.0, 22.4, and 25.5 years. The African-American population has the fewest immigrants or second generation children in the mix, while the Asian and Pacific Islander has the highest proportion foreign born. The Latino population group has the greatest prominence of the second generation.

The California Department of Finance projects the Latino population of California will be 46.8 percent of the total by 2030. In the coming 25 years, immigrants are projected to account for about one-third of working age population growth, while residents of the second generation are projected to account for 59.5 percent of working age population growth, mostly Latinos, who are projected to account for 90.9 percent of the growth in working age population.

Dr Hayes-Bautista (Note 11–4) tells us about California in 2040: "Halfway though her second term, Governor Maria Isabel Rodriguez de Smith mounted the steps of the restored gold-rush era in Sacramento on a crisp November day just before Thanksgiving and loudly rang the bell to announce to all Californians, and to the world, that the state, once again, had lived up to its designation as 'The Golden State'; the California economy of 2040, if considered separately from the rest of the United States, had become the world's second-largest economic unit. The sum total of goods and services generated by the state's productive labor force and entrepreneurs had just surpassed the remaining European competitor. Japan's economy was a distant fifteenth and losing stature; that country had lost more than one third of its population since the millennium, falling from

132 million in 2000 to barely 85 million in 2040. The governor was also pleased to announce that Mexico, for nearly forty years the state's number-one trading partner, had ascended to the number five economic position worldwide."

This rosy picture has a worst case scenario counterpart: Latinos, who are posed to lead in the search for prosperity in California, do not have enough physicians, enough clinics, enough medical knowledge, not even enough health awareness to protect and improve their health.

We have already mentioned our concerns about the increasing disproportion between the minority population and the number of physicians willing to provide services to and in minority communities. We need immediate action to increase interest in health careers among minority students in primary and secondary schools, and in colleges. We also need to support those who choose a medical education and education in other health professions, and need to support the new professionals in their search for excellence.

The current systemic gaps in health care in the State of California and in the U.S. has to be transformed if we aspire to achieve more and have better results.

The San Diego County Medical Society has long advocated for change. In the 1990s, it set forth the following "Prescription for Change" guidelines:

The Prescription for Change:
1. Reduce or eliminate capitation as a form of provider reimbursement.
2. Reconnect consumers to the cost of their day-to-day health care (reduce or eliminate most first dollar insurance coverage).
3. Empower consumers to discover the cost of health care services in advance of consumption.
4. Provide for full tax deductibility of health care expenses for all (including expanding the availability of Medical Savings Accounts).

5. Encourage employer-defined contributions as opposed to employer-defined benefits.
6. Promote private ownership of all health insurance policies.
7. Support mandatory, community-rated, catastrophic health insurance.
8. Require adequate funding mechanisms for the provision of government-mandated services.

BACKGROUND

Quality health care should be uniformly accessible and affordable, and all patients should have the security of knowing they are protected from financial catastrophe as a consequence of major illness or injury.

In San Diego County, health care coverage is neither uniformly accessible nor affordable. In fact, approximately 25 percent of the county's citizens lack health insurance coverage of any kind, with cost being the number one barrier to obtaining coverage. Many physicians believe there has been a very serious decline in access to health care services.

We need to develop public awareness of the precarious condition of the health care delivery system in San Diego.

The San Diego County Medical Society (SDCMS) believes that severe under-funding of the institutions and professions that actually provide front-line care is the root cause of the problems at hand. Physician groups flirt with fiscal insolvency, while many other groups have already failed. San Diego, arguably one of the most attractive places in the nation to live, is unable to offer sufficient wages to attract enough nurses to adequately staff what is now a very reduced number of acute care beds. Hospital systems are closing their smaller community hospitals in order to concentrate assets and to protect the solvency of their core facilities. The county Trauma system is grossly under-funded, with virtually every participating hospital system losing money. The very fabric of San Diego's health care delivery is unraveling just as the baby boomers approach their years of maximum health care utilization.

We must act now to change the way we finance health care before it is too late! Minor adjustments will not correct the problems at hand. In the opinion of the SDCMS council, the situation requires bold intervention and a totally new approach.

Provided herein are eight proposals for change and a brief executive summary of the history and rationale supporting these proposals. The Medical Society intends to take the lead in assembling a coalition that will implement these changes. Our membership must be the driving force behind this effort.

HISTORY OF PRESENT ILLNESS

Prior to and immediately following World War II, most health insurance was high-deductible coverage that protected people against the consequences of extraordinary expenses (catastrophic coverage). Individuals paid their own day-to-day expenses out of pocket (personal funds) and doctors often charged whatever was most appropriate, including such things as accepting payment in chickens or services in kind. The doctor-patient relationship encompassed both the patient's economic status as well as his or her health care needs. The cost of this type of coverage was affordable.

Businesses began to offer health insurance to their employees as an incentive to stay with the company (the birth of the third party payer). Given the affordability of health care at the time, employers gradually began to offer insurance coverage that paid more and more of an employee's total health care costs, including his or her day-to-day expenses. Since 1960, inflation-adjusted per capita spending from personal funds, as a percentage of total spending, has decreased by about 67 percent. While an effective tool for employee retention, disconnecting consumers from the cost of the services they utilize has had very severe unintended consequences.

Premiums began to increase immediately because insurance now needed to cover both the costs of catastrophic illness and the day-to-day expenses of millions of generally healthy people. Employees, no longer connected to the costs, consumed more, as there was little financial consequence to utilizing more advanced or expensive services. Institutions that provided health care services felt free to charge more for their services. Health care prices and consumption rose precipitously, causing the government to ultimately step in to protect the elderly from the resulting health care inflation. This further aggravated the situation by making the government the third party payer of choice for virtually all seniors (Medicare); and worsened the problem by disconnecting the largest per capita consumers of care from the majority of their costs.

The Rand Health Insurance Experiment, funded by the Department of Health & Human Service and reported in 1988, demonstrated beyond any doubt that low deductible insurance that covers first dollar expenses (day-to-day care) increased outpatient expenditures by as much as 67 percent and inpatient spending by nearly 30 percent. Up to that point it had been erroneously theorized that the increased utilization associated with first dollar coverage was the result of sicker people choosing more comprehensive coverage.

Those paying the bills (employers and public agencies) demanded that the rise in insurance premiums be brought under control. The cost controls inherent to a consumer purchasing services with his or her own funds no longer existed in a system of third party payers. Something had to be done to "administratively" replace the missing cost controls. The "gatekeeper" concept and stringent "utilization review" processes were created to restrict access to the more costly forms of care. Unfortunately, these measures had only limited success, primarily because it was difficult for both physicians and patients to justify limiting patient access to care simply because insurance companies wanted to reduce their medical service losses.

Having failed to adequately restrain the rise in health care costs with gatekeeping and utilization review, the insurance industry adopted a new concept for paying providers, *capitation*. Taking advantage of a longstanding rift between primary care providers and specialists, insurers drove a wedge between them by offering the primary care physicians the promise of greater income if they would agree to accept fixed prepayments per patient (capitation). Greater income was to be generated by eliminating wasteful use of expensive services and specialty care. Capitation had another attractive benefit for insurers. It virtually eliminated insurer financial risk by passing on the cost of providing care to the doctors and hospitals. At the rates initially offered, capitation was well received and some savings were initially achieved.

Unfortunately, only large medical groups could afford to accept capitation, as individual physicians could not absorb the cost of even one medical disaster. Patients could no longer be self-directing, as medical groups needed every month's capitation payment to offset the cost of an acute injury or illness when it finally occurred. Insurers, having captured complete control of a large number of capitated lives, began to progressively reduce capitation rates to well below actuarially sound levels. Medical groups, which had now become dependent on these plans, were obliged to accept financially unsound contracts, as rejecting them would result in the immediate loss of all income and bankrupt all but the very strongest groups.

PRESENT DAY CONDITIONS

By its nature, capitation presents an inherent conflict of interest, since the doctors directing patient care ultimately pay for the services rendered. The potential for abuse increases as the actuarial soundness of the capitation rates decrease.

A more insidious consequence of capitation is the gradual loss of access to more advanced services. It is nearly impossible to justify the cost of cutting-edge technology in a system that barely covers present-day expenses. This becomes even more problematic when underfunded medical groups are unable to sub-capitate services unavailable within the group. For hospitals, having surplus capacity clearly works against the bottom line, as it can only result in utilization in excess of capitation payments. As per capita revenue streams decrease, so have the number of hospital beds.

Since the advent of managed care totals, inflation-adjusted per capita health care expenditures have increased by about fifty percent (50%). Few, if any, believe that managed care has increased access to services. Thus, under capitated-managed care, more dollars are being spent than ever before, but consumers have less access to care; leading to the conclusion that the cost of services has actually risen.

From an insurer's standpoint, capitated pre-paid first dollar coverage is a dream come true. Not only are premiums nearly twice as high as conventional catastrophic coverage, but insurers have also managed to retain a similar percentage of the total premium as profit, as if they were still assuming the same degree of financial risk!

It was hoped that first dollar coverage would encourage utilization of preventive health care services, which would then reduce the future incidence of major illness and create a health care dividend to offset the cost of preventive care. Unfortunately, the ratio of catastrophic expenditures to first dollar expenditures has remained remarkably stable over the years and provides little evidence of a significant health care dividend.

As previously discussed, coverage for first dollar expenditures significantly increases the cost of insurance products. Currently, most policies include significant first dollar coverage and premium analysis has shown that first dollar coverage is about 67 percent more expensive than high deductible products (Health Savings Account qualifying insurance). Unfortunately the vast majority of the working uninsured, which includes many minority individuals, were not until recently legally eligible for Health Savings Accounts.

The number one reason given by individuals for not obtaining health insurance and for employers to decline to offer health insurance coverage to their employees is cost. In an attempt to reduce financial barriers to accessing preventive care, we have significantly increased the cost of available insurance products, and have thereby driven nearly one fourth of our citizens out of the insurance pool altogether! The uninsured, no longer participating in the insurance pool, now cost the health care system billions of dollars each year in unfunded federal and state mandated acute care services.

First dollar coverage fosters excess utilization and is, by its nature, much more expensive than true insurance against extraordinary expenses. The public has come to obtain false security from the concept of virtually free health care. In the public's mind, health insurance no longer means protection against extraordinary expenses, but protection against virtually all expenses. Imagine how much auto insurance would cost if it covered every expense including new tires, gasoline, windshield wipers, etc. in addition to the major expenses of accidents?

Finally, employer-sponsored first dollar insurance coverage has spawned a perverse system based on capitation, that operates on the principle of profiting by denying access to health care services.

OVERVIEW OF PROPOSALS

In the United States there are about 187 million insured persons under the age of 65. We believe that it is most rational to design a system of health care financing around the needs of the many. The needs of the exceptions should be addressed separately. Our proposals are interdependent and must be considered as a whole, as alteration or omission of one proposal may significantly impact the effectiveness of another. This is the agenda for the discussion that needs to occur now.

1. Reduce or eliminate capitation as a form of provider reimbursement.

In practice, capitation has actually increased the cost of services and decreased access to care. It is the driving force behind a dangerous trend of progressive dismemberment of the health care infrastructure, just as the boomers approach the age of maximum health care utilization. The Council believes patients and the community are far better served when payments are made for care rendered, not profit from care withheld.

2. Reconnect consumers to the cost of their day-to-day health care (reduce or eliminate most first dollar insurance coverage).

The unintended consequences of first dollar coverage have erased any tangible benefit of increased access for those lucky enough to still have insurance. In contrast, people who are responsible for purchasing their own day-to-day care and who are protected against financial ruin (catastrophic coverage) will shop for more affordable services, and by doing so, will drive down the real cost of services. High deductible coverage is significantly less expensive and more of the uninsured can afford to participate in the insurance pool, thus significantly reducing the amount of unfunded acute care.

The sickest 10 percent of consumers spend about 76 percent of total health care dollars, primarily within acute care facilities. First dollar coverage has not changed that reality. The healthiest 90 percent of the insured population under the age of 65 spends about $500 per year (average less than $42/month) on health and dental care. While an affordable number per person, it represents a total expenditure of about 93.5 billion dollars in excess insurance premiums, not including insurance industry profit and overhead. Paying 93.5 billion dollars for day-to-day care means there is that much less money available for acute care needs.

Finally, when patients pay for a significant portion of their care, they will rightfully demand to choose their own physicianss and the type of care they desire.

3. Empower consumers to discover the cost of health care services in advance of consumption.

Once consumers are reconnected to the cost of their day-to-day care, they must also be empowered to shop more effectively for these services. This means that fee information must be made readily available to consumers in advance of consumption. Once a significant number of patients are reconnected to the cost of their health care, they will demand information on how to access more affordable quality care and web-based information systems will give consumers real-time access to this information. Organized medicine must fight to enable consumers to access free and quality information in an understandable format.

4. Provide for full tax deductibility of health care expenses for all (including expanding the availability of Health Savings Accounts).

The general health of its citizenry is a greater good for the nation as a whole. Encouraging consumers to access necessary care by allowing them to deduct qualified medical expenses and catastrophic health insurance premiums from their tax burden is appropriate and necessary. In addition, enabling consumers to save money in a tax-free environment for future health care needs (Health Savings Accounts) significantly reduces the risk of incurring health expenses that exceed one's ability to pay. A gradual transition from employer tax benefits to individual tax benefits will drive the system toward the individual responsibility we support.

5. Encourage employer-defined contributions as opposed to employer-defined benefits.

Consumers, not employers, must choose the type of coverage they desire. Employers have a business interest in their employees' health. Employer contributions toward a wide array of health care coverage encourage employees to take responsibility and to choose to protect themselves against illness and disability that drives down productivity.

6. Promote private ownership of all health insurance policies.

Individual and families that own their own insurance policies will choose the type of plan that suits their needs and can change jobs without risking a loss of health care coverage.

7. Support mandatory community-rated, catastrophic health insurance.

Like auto liability insurance, mandatory participation in the insurance pool is appropriate and necessary for the benefit of society as a whole. A healthy workforce drives a healthy economy. Community ratings based on age and geographic location enable every individual to obtain protection from financial ruin as a consequence of a major illness or injury. Community rating alone, without a requirement to obtain insurance, could drive up the cost of insurance. A combination of mandated individual coverage and community rating spreads financial risk across the entire population and thus reduces the cost of insurance for those who most need the coverage.

8. Require adequate funding mechanisms for the provision of government-mandated services.

No matter how comprehensive the changes we recommend, some patients will slip through the cracks and appear at hospitals, physicians' offices or other health care treatment facilities without adequate funds to pay for their care. Legislative mandates to provide care must be accompanied by reasonable methods of reimbursing for the care delivered. It is unconscionable for any government agency to mandate the provision of uncompensated care.

The San Diego County Medical Society believes these proposals to be both reasonable and necessary. (Note 11–4).

AMA PROPOSALS (Note 11–5)

AMA coincides with the San Diego Medical Society in proposing modified community rating and guaranteed renewability. The resulting modified community rating, based on age and sex, would have risk ratings and premium variation but in narrower ranges than with individual risk-rating. Average-risk, current group market enrollees would join the new markets, which would provide economies of scale and savings to consumers, thereby reducing administrative expenses and the incentives to risk rate.

Seventy-five percent of policies in the individual market are guaranteed renewable. Insured individuals are likely to remain with the same insurer because the costs of switching outweigh the gains from potentially lower premiums of a different insurer. This should limit premium increases.

Protection against adverse selection could be further enhanced by increasing the insurance funds for high-risk individuals. Additional funds may come from general tax revenues, or may be obtained by providing insurers risk-related subsidies, paid to plans with higher-than-average-risk enrollees by other plans in the market. Another idea is the use of a reinsurance pool for insurers, which would protect against "high spenders."

The marketplace already is responding to pressure for more consumer choice and control of health plans.

This should tend to correct unfair distortions in the current system, expand coverage and choice, and put the patient in control.

AMA PROPOSAL FOR LOW-INCOME PATIENTS

The AMA proposes replacing the joint federal/state financing of the acute medical care portion of the Medicaid program with federal tax credits to individuals (e.g. vouchers for the purchase of health insurance).

Tax credits should be refundable, meaning if patients do not owe taxes, they are still eligible for the credit; *advanceable*, meaning that patients can receive it before the end of the year so that they can pay for coverage; and inversely related to income.

Individuals who would otherwise qualify for Medicaid eligibility groups should receive tax credits that are large enough to enable them to purchase coverage with no cost-sharing.

Low-income individuals who do not qualify for Medicaid should receive tax credits under the same circumstances as above.

Individuals should be allowed to use tax credits to purchase health insurance coverage individually and through programs modeled after state employee purchasing pools or the Federal Employee Health Benefit Program (FEHBP).

For continuity of care, there should be a seamless mechanism to quickly reassess the eligibility group and amount of tax credit with changes in income and family.

HEALTHY PEOPLE 2010

This federal program, initiated in the last years of the 20th Century, provides nation the wide range of opportunities that exist in the present decade. It addresses two challenges: First, we have to make progress in the quality of our lives. Second, we have to make sure that ALL Americans benefit from such advancement.

A CRITICAL LINK TO HEALTHY PEOPLE 2010

The broad-based collaborative between federal, state, and territorial governments, as well hundreds of private, public, and nonprofit organizations, makes *Healthy People 2010*'s mission to prevent disease and promote health by the end of this decade (*www.healthypeople.gov*) a real possibility. This effort has two overarching goals: to increase the quality and years of healthy life and to eliminate health disparities. *Healthy People 2010* features 467 science-based objectives and 10 Leading Health Indicators to help meet its goals.

Progress, according to the program, can be evaluated by the 10 Leading Health Indicators, a set of high-priority public health issues in the United States. The indicators are intended to help everyone more easily understand how healthy we are as a Nation and which are the most important changes we can make to improve our own health as well as the health of our families and communities.

The Leading Health Indicators are:

- Physical Activity
- Overweight and Obesity
- Tobacco Use
- Substance Abuse
- Responsible Sexual Behavior
- Mental Health
- Injury and Violence
- Environmental Quality
- Immunization
- Access to Health Care

Each indicator will be tracked, measured and reported on regularly throughout the decade.

SEEING THE WHOLE PICTURE

Each Leading Health Indicator is an important health issue by itself. Together, the set of indicators helps us understand that there are many factors that matter to the health of individuals, communities and the nation. Each of the indicators depends to some extent on:

- The information people have about their health and how to make improvements
- Choices people make (behavioral factors)
- Where and how people live (environmental, economic and social conditions)
- The type, amount and quality of health care people receive (access to health care and characteristics of the healthcare system)

Realizing improvements for the set of indicators will require effective public and private sector programs that address multiple factors.

MAKING CONNECTIONS ACROSS INDICATORS

Identifying changes to improve any one of the Leading Health Indicators is good; identifying changes that will cut across and improve several indicators simultaneously is also important. Thinking "outside the indicator" means that we can look at how one contributing factor or one important change may affect several indicators. The indicators can also provide the foundation for new partnerships across health issues and new thinking about how to address the many health concerns we face.

An example of this type of innovative thinking is collaboration among those who want to increase the amount of physical activity individuals do and promote weight loss to reach a healthy weight. Other cross-cutting action ideas are:

- *Combining education for parents into a "healthy home" program that addresses injury prevention, nutrition, and the impact of environmental tobacco smoke on children and other family members.*
- *Designing worksite wellness programs to address several indicators simultaneously, such as physical activity, overweight and obesity, and tobacco use.*
- *Using existing communications and outreach efforts for immunization to promote enrollment of children in health insurance programs.*

In short, the Leading Health Indicators can be a tool to develop comprehensive health activities that work simultaneously to improve many aspects of health.

TAKING ACTION TO IMPROVE EVERYONE'S HEALTH

The Leading Health Indicators are intended to motivate citizens and communities to take actions to improve the health of individuals, families, communities and the nation. The indicators can help us determine *what each one of us can do and where we can best focus our energies*—at home, and in our communities, worksites, businesses, or states—to live better and longer.

Some possible actions are to:

- *Adopt the 10 Leading Health Indicators as personal and professional guides for choices about how to make health improvements.*
- *Encourage public health professionals and public officials to adopt the Leading Health Indicators as the basis for public health priority-setting and decision-making.*
- *Urge our public and community health systems and our community leadership to use the Leading Health Indicators as measures of local success for investments in health improvements.*

FEDERAL RESOURCES

More information on the Leading Health Indicators, including links to Federal websites with data, planning tools, scientific information, and details about various programs are available at *www.healthypeople.gov/LHI.*

In this book we have explored the problems presented by a great number of patients with different backgrounds, places of origin, physical characteristics, and perceptions of health care. There are, we feel, some key points to reflect upon and take with you:

Appearances are deceiving. A Latino born in Cuba and living in the United States may still follow a culture that may be less firmly entrenched in the island. His children and grand-children may share more genetic factors with the non-Latino population of the United States than with Cubans that still reside on the island. Explicit genetic data, rather than place of origin, may resolve questions about genetic factors in illness and health.

People and cultures change. No culture is static, and successive generations of the same family may preserve different values and traditions. A generalization about a cultural group is good in the initial exploration of helpful ideas, but absolute generalizations tend to be wrong.

Within a community that coexists with others, each individual has cultural choices. Time and again we have seen a family fluctuate among different cultures, and finally acquire a unique character.

"Geographic ancestry" is a concept that may bridge the gap between genetic and cultural considerations. In California and in other places where Latinos, Asians, African-Americans and others look for identifying factors that may be a personal source of pride, and for commonalities to be used for shared goals, the flexibility provided by new concepts may be a welcome step towards more progress in community building.

Old and new concepts have a place in the debate about disparities in health. What is most critical is to generate testable hypotheses, and fund the community research necessary to test them.

APPENDIX A

Here are the members of the Black Caucus, to whom we owe a great deal of gratitude:

OFFICERS

Member of Congress	State
Rep. Melvin L. Watt, Chair	North Carolina
Rep. Corrine Brown, Vice-Chair	Florida
Rep. Carolyn Kilpatrick, Second Vice-Chair	Michigan
Rep. Danny K. Davis, Secretary	Illinois
Rep. Barbara Lee, Whip	California

MEMBERS

Member of Congress	State
Rep. Sanford D. Bishop, Jr.	Georgia
Rep. G.K. Butterfield	North Carolina
Rep. Julia M. Carson	Indiana
Rep. Donna M. Christian-Christensen	Virgin Islands
Rep. William L. Clay, Jr.	Missouri
Rep. Emanuel Cleaver, II	Missouri
Rep. James E. Clyburn	South Carolina

APPENDIX A

Rep. John Conyers, Jr. (founding member)	Michigan
Rep. Elijah E. Cummings	Maryland
Rep. Artur Davis	Alabama
Rep. Chaka Fattah	Pennsylvania
Rep. Harold E. Ford, Jr.	Tennessee
Rep. Al Green	Texas
Rep. Alcee L. Hastings	Florida
Rep. Jesse L. Jackson, Jr.	Illinois
Rep. Sheila Jackson Lee	Texas
Rep. William J. Jefferson	Louisiana
Rep. Eddie Bernice Johnson	Texas
Rep. Stephanie Tubbs Jones	Ohio
Rep. John Lewis	Georgia
Rep. Cynthia McKinney	Georgia
Rep. Kendrick Meek	Florida
Rep. Gregory W. Meeks	New York
Rep. Juanita Millender-McDonald	California
Rep. Gwen Moore	Wisconsin
Rep. Eleanor Holmes Norton	Washington, D.C.
Sen. Barack Obama	Illinois
Rep. Major R. Owens	New York
Rep. Donald M. Payne	New Jersey
Rep. Charles B. Rangel (founding member)	New York
Rep. Bobby L. Rush	Illinois
Rep. David Scott	Georgia
Rep. Robert C. Scott	Virginia
Rep. Bennie G. Thompson	Mississippi
Rep. Edolphus Towns	New York
Rep. Maxine Waters	California
Rep. Diane E. Watson	California
Rep. Melvin L. Watt	North Carolina
Rep. Albert R. Wynn	Maryland

Congressional Hispanic Caucus Office:

1609 Longworth HOB
Washington, DC 20515
Phone: (202) 225-2410
Fax: (202) 225-0027

Here are the members of the Hispanic Caucus:

Hon. Grace Napolitano (CA-38)
Chair
Longworth House Office Building
Washington, DC 20515
Phone (202) 225-5256
Fax: (202) 225-0027
Resources Committee
Small Business Committee

Hon. Joe Baca (CA-43)
1st Vice Chair
House Office Building
Washington, D.C. 20515-0542
Phone: (202) 225-6161
Fax: (202) 225-8671
Agriculture Committee
Science Committee

Hon. Raul Grijalva (CA-18)
2nd Vice Chair
1440 Longworth HOB
Washington, DC 20515
Phone: (202)225-2435
Fax: (202)225-1541
Committee on Education
    Workforce
Committee on Resources

Hon. Lucille Roybal-Allard (CA-34)
Whip
30 Rayburn House Office Building
Washington, DC 20515
(202) 225-1766
(202) 226-0350 fax
Appropriations Committee

Hon. Xavier Becerra (CA-31)
1119 Longworth House Office
  Building
Washington, DC 20515
(202) 225-6235
(202) 225-2202 fax
Ways and Means Committee

Hon. Dennis Cardoza (CA-18)
435 Cannon Building
Washington, DC 20515
Office Hours: 8:30 to 5:30 EST
Monday through Friday
(202) 225-6131
Fax: 225-0819
800-356-6424
Committee on Resources
House Committee on Agriculture
Committee on International
  Relations

Hon. Jim Costa (CA-20)
1004 Longworth House Office
  Building
Washington, DC 20515
Phone: 202-225-3341
Fax: 202-225-9308
Resources Committee.
House Agriculture Committee
House Committee on Science

Hon. Henry Cuellar (TX-28)
1404 Longworth House Office
  Building
Washington, DC 20515
Phone: 202-225-1640
Fax: 202-225-1641

Hon. Charles A. Gonzalez (TX-20)
327 Cannon House Office
  Building
Washington, DC 20515
(202) 225-3236
(202) 225-1915 fax
Banking & Financial Services
  Committee
Small Business Committee

Hon. Luis V. Gutieriez (IL-4)
2367 Rayburn Building
Washington, DC 20515
Phone: (202) 225-8203
Fax: (202) 225-7810

Hon. Ruben Hinojosa (TX-15)
1032 Longworth House Office
  Building
Washington, DC 20515
(202) 225-2531
(202) 225-5688 fax
Education and the Workforce
  Committee
Small Business Committee

Hon. Robert Menendez (NJ)
405 Cannon House Office
  Building
Washington, DC 20515
(202) 225-7919
(202) 226-0792 fax
International Relations Committee
Transportation & Infrastructure
  Committee

Hon. Solomon Ortiz (TX-27)
2136 Rayburn House Office
    Building
Washington, DC 20515
(202) 225-7742
(202) 226-1134 fax
Armed Services Committee
    Resources Committee

Hon. Ed Pastor (AZ-4)
2465 Rayburn House Office
    Building
Washington, DC 20515
(202) 225-4065
(202) 225-1655 fax
Appropriations Committee
Standards and Ethics Committee

Hon. Silvestre Reyes (TX-18)
514 Cannon House Office
    Building
Washington DC 20515
Phone: (202) 225-4831
Fax: (202) 225-2016
Armed Serviced Committee
Veterans' Affairs Committee

Hon. John Salazar (CO-3)
1531 Longworth HOB
Washington, DC 20515
Phone: (202)-225-4761
Fax: (202)-226-9669
House Committee on Agriculture

Hon. Linda Sanchez (CA-39)
1007 Longworth Building
Washington, DC 20515
Phone: (202) 225-6676
Fax: (202) 226-1012

Hon. Loretta Sanchez (CA-47)
1529 Longworth House Office
    Building
Washington, DC 20515
(202) 225-2965
(202) 226-0341 fax
Education and the Workforce
    Committee
Armed Services Committee

Hon. Jose Serrano (NY-16)
2342 Rayburn House Office
    Building
Washington, DC 20515
(202) 225-4361
(202) 225-6001 fax
Appropriations Committee

Hon. Hilda Solis (CA-32)
    1725 Longworth House Office
    Building
Washington, DC   20515
Phone: (202) 225-5464
Fax: (202) 225-5467
House Committee on Energy and
    Commerce

Hon. Nydia Velazquez (NY-12)
2241 Rayburn House Office
    Building
Washington, DC 20515
Phone: (202) 225-2361
Fax: (202) 226-0327
Banking & Financial Services
    Committee
Small Business Committee

NOTES

NOTES FOR CHAPTER ONE

Note 1–1. Phimister, E. "Medicine and the Racial Divide" *N. Engl J Med*. 348: 1081–1082, 2003.

Note 1–2. Golden, K.M. "Voodoo in Africa and the United States." *Am. J. Psychiatry* 134: 1425–1427, 1977.

Note 1–3. *The Economist: World in Figures*, 2004 Edition. London, U.K.: Profile Books.

Note 1–4. Pennisi, E. "Speaking in Tongues" *Science* 303: 1321–1323, 2004.

Note 1–5. The WHO World Mental Health Survey Consortium. "Prevalence, Severity, and Unmet Need for Treatment of Mental Disorders in the World Health Organization World Mental Health Surveys." *JAMA* 291: 2581–2590, 2004. *(This excellent source of information gives much food for thought. There is a crying need for reallocation of funds, so the most effective use of scarce results can be obtained.)*

Note 1–6. Health Resources and Services Administration (HRSA). "Cultural Competence Works: Using Cultural Competence to Improve the Quality of Care for Diverse Populations and Add Value to Managed Care Arrangements" *HRSA, 2001.*

Note 1–7. Katz, D.L. "Representing Your Community in Community-based Participatory Research: Differences Made and Measured." *Preventing Chronic Disease* No. 1, January 2004.

Note 1–8. Ad Hoc Committee on Health Literacy for the Council on Scientific Affairs, "AMA Health Literacy: Report of the Council on Scientific Affairs." *JAMA* 281: 552–557, 1999.

Note 1–9. APA. "Final Report: APA Task Force on Quality Indicators." 1999.

NOTES FOR CHAPTER TWO

NOTE 2–1. Villaseñor, V. *Burro Genius*. New York: HarperCollins Publishers, 2004. The acclaimed writer lives in California on the ranch where he grew up. He is the author of numerous best-selling works.

NOTE 2–2. Munoz, R.A., Boddy, P., et al. "Depression in the Hispanic Community." *Annals of Clinical Psychiatry*. 2:115–120, 1990.

NOTE 2–3. Kadushin, C. *Why People Go to Psychiatrists*. New York: Atherton Press, 1969.

NOTES ON CHAPTER THREE

NOTE 3–1. This quotation from Alfred Alvarez, the quotation from Dorothy Parker and the information about Ambrose Bierce, are all taken from the book *On Suicide: Great Writers on the Ultimate Question*, (San Francisco: Chronicle Books, 1992) edited by John Miller.

NOTES ON CHAPTER FOUR

NOTE 4 –.1..Ruth became involved in one of the numerous studies conducted years ago to validate the diagnostic criteria developed by Washington University, in St. Louis, Missouri, which in turn became the basis of the criteria for the major psychiatric disorders included in DSM-III. At that time, some clinicians could have described Ruth's symptoms as one of disassociation, even though Ruth was always aware of her different behaviors.

NOTE 4–2. Evidence indicating that carbohydrate metabolism may be impaired in patients with schizophrenia and other psychiatric disorders has been around for longer than fifty years. We continue to be diligent readers of the many theories that explain this problem. Our first paper on the subject (Schwarz, L. and Munoz, R. "Blood Sugar Levels in Patients Treated with Chlorpromazine." *American Journal of Psychiatr.*.125: 149–51, 1968.) started with the observation described in this chapter. Since then we have spent much time trying to develop initiatives to prevent high blood sugar among our patients with mental disorders.

NOTES ON CHAPTER FIVE

NOTE 5–1. Many recent papers have focused on alcohol metabolism and minorities. Gene polymorphism may be a clue to the enormous variance in addictive tendencies among different groups. *See* Wall, T.L, Carr, L.G., et al. "Protective Association of Genetic Variation in Alcohol Dehydrogenase with Alcohol Dependence in Native American Mission Indians." *Am J Psychiat.* 160: 41–46, 2003.

NOTE 5–2. The neuroanatomical substrates of drug abuse are increasingly better studied. Today we have firm bases to talk about addictions as diseases of the brain. *See* Cami, J. and Farre, M. "Drug Addiction." *NEJM.* 349: 975–986, 2003.

NOTE 5–3. Naltrexone continues to be relevant to any study of proper management of drug addiction among minorities. *See* Fuller, R.K. and Gordis, E. "Naltrexone Treatment for Alcohol Dependence." *NEJM.* 345: 1770–1771, 2001.

NOTE 5–4. Recent papers support the combination of Naltrexone with psychotherapy for patients with alcoholism. *See* Anton, R. F., Moak, D.H., et al. "Naltrexone and Cognitive Behavioral Therapy for the Treatment of Outpatient Alcoholics: Results of a Placebo-Controlled Trial." *Focus.* 183–189, 2003.

NOTE 5–5. Proper application of current knowledge permits most physicians to offer help to addicted persons during withdrawal. See Kasten, T.R. and O'Connor, P.G. "Management of Drug and Alcohol Withdrawal." *NEJM.* 348: 1786–1795, 2003.

NOTE 5–6. Strain, E.C., Stitzer, M.L., et al. "Comparison of Buprenorphine and Methadone in the Treatment of Opioid Dependence." *Am J Psychiat.* 151: 1025–1030, 1994.

NOTES ON CHAPTER SIX

NOTE 6–1. A number of psychotherapists have noted that psychotherapy should always be oriented towards the future. Bernard D. Beitman, chair of the Department of Psychiatry at the University of Missouri at Columbia, has been a major advocate of this position. He and his colleagues have recently summarized their thoughts in this regard.

Beitman, B.D., Soth, A.M., Good, G.E. "Integrating Psychotherapy Through an Emphasis on the Future: A Case Study" (in press).

NOTE 6–2. Problems like the ones suffered by Vickie have been a major target for Cognitive Therapy. From the pioneer work of Aaron Beck, M.D., to the recent application of its tenets to most psychiatric problems, Cognitive Therapy continues to be one of our most useful therapeutic tools. Dr. David Burns, a protégé of Dr. Beck, has written a book that is one of the most popular on this subject. Burns, D.D. *Feeling Good: The New Mood Therapy.* New York: Avon Books, 1999.

NOTE 6–3. Interpersonal Psychotherapy is second only to Cognitive Therapy in its multiple applications. The applications continue to expand in the practice of psychiatry. Transitions, losses, and conflicts receive proper attention in this form of psychotherapy.

Klerman, G.L. and Weissman, M.M. *Applications of Interpersonal Psychotherapy.* Washington, DC: American Psychiatric Press Inc., 1993.

NOTE 6–4. Among the many manuals currently in existence, our favorite, because it is simple and effective, is by Babior and Goldman. Babior, S. and Goldman, C. *Overcoming Panic Anxiety and Phobias.* Duluth, MN: Whole Person Associates, 1995.

NOTE 6–5. Compared to today's mammoth textbooks of psychiatry, Dr. Viktor Frankl's *Man's Search for Meaning* is the most practical, most influential small book. Surprising for psychiatric books, it has gone through numerous editions, printings, and appearances, and continues to be influential, especially among those who appreciate quality rather than quantity. We hesitate to recommend any edition. They are all basically the same.

NOTE 6–6. We appreciate authors who review a theme and write a paper that is comprehensive, factual, and readable. We found one. Bustillo, J.R., Lauriello, J., Horan, W.P., and Keith, S.J. "The Psychosocial Treatment of Schizophrenia: An Update." *American Journal of Psychiatry*, 158: 163–175, 2001.

NOTE 6–7. In this case, the facts speak louder than any further explanation. Well K, Klap R, et al.: "Ethnic Disparities in Unmet Need for Alcoholism, Drug Abuse, and Mental Health Care." *American Journal of Psychiatry.* 158: 2027–2032, 2001.

NOTE 6–8. Considering the substantial prevalence of drug dependence among patients with other psychiatric disorders, any treatment will fail if it only addresses one disorder. Remission among people with drug dependence who are also treated for other psychiatric disorders is higher than expected. Those who are actively using drugs while seeking treatment for the other psychiatric disorder pose the big challenge. Dixon, L., McNary, S, et al. "Remission of Substance Use Disorder among Psychiatric Inpatients with Mental Illness." *American Journal of Psychiatry.* 155(2): 239–243, 1998.

NOTE 6–9. Albert Gaw, ethnic minority psychiatrists who has written extensively about cultural issues, summarized the report on substance abuse prevention for the *American Journal of Psychiatry.* Gaw, J.C. "Substance

Abuse Prevention in Multicultural Communities." (book review). *American Journal of Psychiatry*. 156: 1289, 1999.

NOTE 6–10. The best way not to see the ethnic minorities is not to count them. We have to be prepared to question findings that reflect the problems and the aspirations of others. Humphreys, K. and Weisner, C. "Use of Exclusion Criteria in Selecting Research Subjects and its Effect on the Generalizability of Alcohol Treatment Studies." *American Journal of Psychiatry*. 157: 588–594, 2000.

NOTES FOR CHAPTER SEVEN

NOTE 7–1. Dr. Wonodi, one of our consultants, discussed several of the difficulties involved in analyzing Olo's response to treatment:

> The fact that both risperidone and 9–OH-risperidone levels were low suggests that Olo's case might have been complicated by other reasons. A) Was treatment non-adherence an issue? (given his hostile response to the resident, this cannot be totally ruled out, even though his response to the question might be explained by the paranoia expected in a non-responder. One also wonders if the appropriately timed clinical confrontation by the resident, and the conference, which would have recruited the active participation of his immediate family and those at home (he was not working, thus not earning an income, and probably not able to send money home, too) led to improved treatment adherence on the part of Olo. B) Were there herbal medications in the picture? There is a growing body of literature on herb-drug interactions that could be in the service of efficacy, lack of efficacy, or the emergence of adverse events. This would be an important factor in a person of African descent who is a first generation immigrant who kept in touch with his family back in Nigeria, and sent money home for education of family members. Did he also send money home for the purchase of herbal remedies, which can easily be brought over by a visiting family member, or friend? C) Though far-fetched, is it possible that this was also a case of psychotic depression given the good premorbid level of function, education, marital status, and response to addition of paroxetine?

NOTE 7–2. Caraco, Y. "Genes and the Response to Drugs." *NEJM*. 351: 2867–2869, 2004.

NOTE 7–3. Ruiz, P., ed.. *Ethnicity and Psychopharmacology*. Washington, DC: American Psychiatric Press, 2000.

NOTE 7–4. Many patients who have lost their hearing over a long period become expert lip readers. We tested fifty patients in our office, using a hand-held audioscope combined with an audiometer. Five (10%) had lost perception for 40 dB at 2000 Hz in both ears and clearly needed a hearing aid. None wanted it (*See* Munoz, R.A. "Can Our Patients Hear?" *Annals of Clinical Psychiatry*. 3: 115–118, 1991.).

NOTE 7–5. Pi, E.H. and Simpson, G.M. "Cross-cultural Psychopharmacology: A Current Clinical Perspective." *Psychiatric Services*. 56: 31–33, 2005.

NOTES FOR CHAPTER EIGHT

NOTE 8–1. As we were searching for ideas about the rapid transformation of groups of people who come to the United States, *Smithsonian* published several articles that responded to the questions we were asking:

Marc Kaufman presented the bases for our section on the Hmong people in his article, "American Odyssey," (*Smithsonian*. September 2004, 85–91). The facts were kept alive and dramatic by Kaufman's wonderful style.

NOTE 8–2. For a number of years, we have appreciated the efforts of the colleagues in the Cuban community in Miami to try to understand and describe in scientific terms the many aspects of the Cuban migration to the United States.

The Institute for Cuban and Cuban-American Studies at the University of Miami published, in August 2004, the report on which we based this section of Chapter 8:

"*Value Orientations and Opinions of Recently Arrived Cubans in Miami.*" (Principal investigators: Dr. Andy S. Gomez and Dr. Eugenio M. Rothe; Co-Investigators: Dr. Frank Mora, Dr. Hector Castillo-Matos, Dr. John Lewis; Project Consultants: Dr. Juan Clark, Ramon Colas.) *Thank you, Eugenio, for continuing to share your work with us.*

NOTE 8–3. There are community leaders who live their role with elegance, distinction, and the bearing of those destined to direct other people. That was the case of our friend Danneta. We were surprised when she told us she had been born in the poor, segregated area reserved for African Americans in a town of southern New Mexico. When she showed us her family album, it was full of equally distinguished professionals and leaders who had come from their little town to occupy key positions elsewhere.

Danetta visited us when she came back from a class reunion for her segregated primary school in Hobbs, New Mexico. She had told Dr.

Charles Becknell about our conversations, and he had sent us a copy of his autobiography. He had added a nice personal note. We hope to meet Dr. Becknell in person. (Becknell, C. E. *No Challenge–No Change: Growing up Black in New Mexico*. Kearny, NE: Jubilee Publications, 2003.)

NOTE 8–4. Also in the *Smithsonian* issue from September 2004 (50–65) were three excellent articles on Native Americans. They honored the first museum to open on the National Mall in seventeen years, the National Museum of the American Indian. The museum opening, attended by an estimated 25,000 Native Americans, was a tribute to the resilience, optimism, and vigor of the oldest American people.

We obtained ideas from the incredible array of information available at the museum. Most of the 800,000 artifacts and 125,000 historical photographs came from the vast collection assembled by New Yorker George Gustav Heye, in the first part of the last century.

Also on occasion of the museum opening, *U.S. News & World Report* devoted its section on "Science & Society" to the "Modern Life of the Native Americans" (October 4, 2004, 46–54), which provided much information for Chapter 8.

NOTE 8–5. Many members of the U.S. House of Representatives have often opened their doors to us. Bob Filner and Susan Davis, both in Congress from San Diego, have always been enormously generous with their time. Xavier Becerra, then chair of the Hispanic Caucus, and several members of the Caucus spent a delightful evening with us. They showed their strong commitment to mental health and to universal health care.

See Appendix A for a list of officers and other members of the Congressional Black Caucus, as of this writing.

See Appendix B for a list of officers and other members of the Congressional Hispanic Caucus, as of this writing.

NOTE 8–6. Becknell, C. E. *No Challenge—No Change: Growing up Black in New Mexico*. Kearny, NE: Jubilee Publications, 2003.

NOTES FOR CHAPTER TEN

NOTE 10–1. Smedley, B.D., Stith A.Y., and Nelson, A.R. "Unequal Treatment: Confronting Racial and Ethnic Disparities in Health Care." Washington, DC: National Academy Press, 2002.

NOTE 10–2. AMA. "Report of the Council on Scientific Affairs: Racial and Ethnic Disparities in Health Care," 2003. We are grateful to Dr. Carolyn Rabinowitz, our advocate as a member of the council, for her numerous ideas and actions in behalf of the ethnic minorities.

NOTE 10–3. Cooper, R.S., Kaufman, J.S., and Ward, R. "Race and Genomics." *New England Journal of Medicine*, 348(12): 1166–1170, March 20, 2003.

NOTE 10–4. Sankar, P., Cho, M.K., Condit, C.M., et al. "Genetic Research and Health Disparities." *Journal of the American Medical Association*, 291: 2985–2989, 2004.

NOTE 10–5. Wong, M.D., Shapiro, M.F., et al. "Contribution of Major Disease to Disparities in Mortality." *New England Journal of Medicine*, 347: 1585–1592, 2003.

NOTE 10–6. Sehgal, A.R. "Impact of Quality Improvement Efforts on Race and Sex Disparities in Hemodialysis." *Journal of the American Medical Association*, 289: 996–1000, 2003.

NOTE 10–7. Cooper, R.S., Kaufman, J.S., and Ward, R. "Race and Genomics."

NOTE 10–8. United States General Accounting Office. "Physician Workforce: Physician Supply Increased in Metropolitan Areas, but Geographic Disparities Persisted," October 2003.

NOTE 10–9. Health Resources and Services Administration. "Comments to Physician Workforce: Physician Supply Increased in Metropolitan Areas, but Geographic Disparities Persisted," October 2003.

NOTE 10–10. Cooper R.A. "Shortage of Doctors Predicted." *Annals of Internal Medicine*, 141: 705–714, 732–734, 2004.

NOTES ON THE EPILOGUE

NOTE 11–1. Hayes-Bautista, D.E., *La Nueva California. Latinos in the Golden State*, University of California Press. Berkeley, 2004

NOTE 11–2. The American Academy of Family Physicians (AAFP), the American College of Physicians (ACP), and the American Psychiatric Association (APA) represent the nation's three largest physician groups that diagnose and treat patients with depressive disorders. To enhance clinical management of depression, the three societies have teamed up to engage primary care and psychiatric practices in developing practice-driven strategies to improve management of depression in routine clinical practice. Primary aims of this collaborative initiative are to: 1) assess the clinical utility of a simple quantitative instrument to measure the severity of depression, and 2) test office systems and management strategies that optimize monitoring of depression in routine clinical practice. Such a tool has the added benefits of:

- Making medication and clinical management more time efficient.
- Providing a standardized approach for monitoring depression, suicidality, and response to treatment for patients receiving antidepressants.
- Providing documentation of patient need for treatment.
- Providing a common language for cross-specialty communication about depression severity, therapeutic response, etc.

Interest in a brief quantitative rating instrument was inspired in part by the established practice of monitoring blood pressure to treat hypertension. The societies' representatives agreed to study the usefulness of a comparable approach for monitoring depression severity. For this collaborative project, the nine-item, patient-reported *Patient Health Questionnaire (PHQ-9)* best meet the criteria for a depression screening and severity measurement tool. This instrument is currently being used in the Federal Bureau of Primary Care National Collaboratives, The MacArthur Foundation Depression Toolkit, and the New York City Department of Health Wellness Initiative, as well as in many HMO's in the U.S.

Collaborative Description: Eighteen practices have been initially selected to represent the breadth of outpatient psychiatric practice types. An additional 18 practices representing primary care will be selected among network members of the AAFP and the ACP to take part in this National Depression Management Leadership collaborative project.

Using the principles of **participatory research** (in which all participants are both learners and researchers) and combining strategies pioneered by the *Institute for Healthcare Improvement Breakthrough Series*, practices will form improvement teams within each site and work with project faculty to identify, test, and implement improvements in depression management during the course of the project. Although this project will focus on improving depression management, the fundamental change processes can be applicable to other psychiatric conditions. As a part of this collaborative, practices are asked to:

1. Complete pre-work activities including collecting information on practice, structure and composition, and selecting Improvement Team members.
2. Identify two members of the Improvement Team (a physician and office staff/nurse) to participate in three, two-day Learning Sessions. Sessions were held April 8–10, June 24–26, and November 4–6 of 2005 in Chicago.
3. Test innovations in the management of depression during three Action

Phases (following each of the three Learning Sessions) using rapid cycle change concepts. Participants will be asked to join conference calls during Action Phases to help solve logistical problems and to share successes.

The Learning Sessions provide opportunities for practice participants to share experiences and plan the testing of new innovations in their practices during the subsequent Action Phases. Sessions for primary care physicians and psychiatrists will be held simultaneously, with several combined segments as well as sessions tailored to the unique needs of each specialty. Evidence-based concepts of improving depression care and practical approaches to use of follow-up files, decision supporting varying stages of treatment, care management, and patient self-management education will be reviewed. Rapid cycle testing of innovations will be introduced and discussed for use in the Action Phases.

NOTE 11–3. Myers, D., Pitkin J. and Park J. "California Demographic Futures. Projections to 2030, by Immigrant Generations, Native, and Time of Arrival in U. S." School of Policy, Planning, and Development. University of Southern California, 2005.

NOTE 11–4. (References)

1. Willard G. Manning, Joseph P. Newhouse, Naihua Duan, Emmett Keeler, Bernadette Benjamin, Arlene Leibowitz, M. Susan Marquis, Jack Zwanziger, R-3476–HHS, "Health Insurance and the Demand For Medical Care", February 1988; The Rand Corporation (Supported by a grant from the U.S. Department of Health and Human Services).

2. Katharine R. Levit, Helen C. Lazenby, Bradley R. Braden, and the National Health Accounts Team, "National Health Spending Trends In 1996", *Health Affairs*, January/February 1998.

3. Mark L. Berk and Alan C. Monheit, "The Concentration of Health Expenditures: An Update", *Health Affairs*, Winter 1992.

NOTE 11–5. Palmisano, D.J., Emmons D.W., Wozniak, G.D.: "Expanding Insurance Coverage Through Tax Credits, Consumer Choice, and Market Enhancements" *JAMA*. 291: 2237–2256, 2004.

INDEX

addictive behavior. *See* drug addiction

advocates for ethnic minority health
  care, 183–186
  clinics for Latinos, 184–185
  David E. Hayes-Bautista, 184
  Francis Lu, 187
  Jeanne Spurlock, 187–188
  primary physicians, 191–193
  psychiatrists (minority), 187–188
  Ruben Martinez, 189–190
  support center in the community,
    190–191

African Americans. *See also* ethnic
  minorities
  alcoholism and, 81–82
  attitude towards mental illness,
    155–156
  family life of, 154–156
  lithium and, 115–116
  personal narrative (Dr. Charles E.
    Becknell), 130–134
  political power and, 136–141
  psychopharmacology and,
    113–117

aging. *See* old age

AIDs, personal narrative, 121–123

alcoholism. *See also* drug addiction
  addictions and the brain, 80
  Asian Americans and, 82
  factors that influence, 80–82
  genetic susceptibility to, 73–75
  nature vs. nurture as cause of, 81
  personal narratives, 73–75, 80–82
  psychotherapy and, 102–103
  therapeutic agents to help treat,
    80, 82–84

alpha glycoprotein, 116

Alzheimer's disease
  depression and, 53–55
  forgetting to speak English, 54
  personal narrative, 66–67
  psychosis and, 66–67

American Medical Association
  (AMA)
  proposal to improve health care
    insurance, 205–207

antidepressants, 112, 113
  side effects from 124

antipsychotic medications, overweight patients and, 70–71